Tax Administrations and Capacity Building

A COLLECTIVE CHALLENGE

Please cite this publication as:
OECD (2016), *Tax Administrations and Capacity Building: A Collective Challenge*, OECD Publishing, Paris.
http://dx.doi.org/10.1787/9789264256637-en

ISBN 978-92-64-25662-0 (print)
ISBN 978-92-64-25663-7 (PDF)

Corrigenda to OECD publications may be found on line at: *www.oecd.org/about/publishing/corrigenda.htm*.

Preface

This report is published at a time when the international community has sharpened its focus on the importance of building tax capacity across nations to help achieve objectives related to the 2030 Agenda for Sustainable Development and the G20's tax agenda. The confluence of these agendas is resulting in increasing demands for experts and investments and, in a context of finite resources, requires tax administrations to examine their role and contributions. It also creates an imperative to innovate and better collaborate to achieve the broader goal of strengthening tax administration globally.

Over the past several months, we have been working to advance the work of a capacity building project that was launched through the OECD Forum on Tax Administration. This work has culminated in a report that proposes a way forward for the FTA and its member countries to organise individual and collective capacity building efforts in a more co-ordinated, cost-effective and strategic way.

As sponsors of the FTA Capacity Building Project, we are confident the recommendations proposed in the report will lay the ground work for more focused and impactful collaboration in the future. Moving forward, we would like to underscore the importance of sound diagnostics and measurement of results to assist and inform decision making. An evidence-based approach will help tax administrations focus their resources on investments that are likely to yield the greatest results.

As this work progresses, we remain mindful of the need to ensure that the results of our work are accessible to developing country tax administrations whose priorities and circumstances vary widely and must be considered. The recommendations in the report relating to the Knowledge Sharing Platform and better connecting to the work of others are particularly relevant in enabling the broader sharing and dissemination of our collective investments to the benefit of all.

This report presents an opportunity for the tax administration community more broadly to reflect on the need to undertake capacity building in a manner that is more targeted, strategic, and effective. Going forward, we look forward to collaborating with partners to support this important priority.

Mr. Andrew Treusch
Commissioner
Canada Revenue Agency
Canada

Mr. Wang Jun
Commissioner
State Administration of Taxation
China

Foreword

The Forum on Tax Administration

Effective tax systems are a critical building block for increased domestic resource mobilisation which is essential for sustainable development, promoting self-reliance, good governance, growth and stability, with particular relevance to developing countries.

At the same time, the move to the implementation of the G20 tax priorities has pushed tax co-operation to unprecedented levels, with various international stakeholders assisting developing countries in building their tax capacity.

This study is based on the outcome of a mapping exercise and a survey of ***members of the Forum on Tax Administration*** (FTA) and draws on the insights and expertise of a nine-country task team. It is intended to offer guidance as to how the FTA and its member countries can best organise themselves to contribute to capacity building efforts in a co-ordinated and cost-effective way as to complement, not duplicate, ongoing work in capacity building, both in relation to G20 priorities and more generally.

> The Forum on Tax Administration (FTA) was formed in 2002 as a subsidiary body of the OECD Committee on Fiscal Affairs. Since then, it has grown to become a unique forum for co-operation between revenue bodies at Commissioner-level with participation from 46 jurisdictions. The vision for the FTA is to establish a forum through which tax administrators can identify, discuss and influence relevant global trends and develop new ideas to enhance tax administration around the world.
>
> The work programme of the FTA is directed and overseen by a Bureau comprised of commissioners from 13 revenue bodies. The FTA's work on tax administration is published in the form of reports and guidance notes and is widely referenced and used by members and the broader tax community. The FTA also publishes the OECD's Tax Administration Series, a biennial report that provides comparative information and data on tax administrations across 56 advanced and emerging economies (including all OECD, EU, and G20 members).
>
> By providing a forum to meet and work collaboratively on global tax administration challenges, share best practices, and identify new opportunities for taking collective action to achieve common goals, the FTA enables revenue bodies to increase the efficiency, effectiveness and fairness of tax administration. More information on the FTA, including details on products and publications, can be found at its website: www.oecd.org/tax/fta.

This study is part of the OECD Tax Administration Information and Guidance Series, which extends across a range of areas of key interest to revenue bodies. National revenue bodies differ in a number of important ways, including in respect of their institutional legacies, the tax systems they administer, and the broader context they are part of.

The series is therefore intended to inspire and inform revenue bodies rather than promote a standard approach to tax administration, which may be neither practical nor desirable. Inquiries concerning this study should be directed to the International Co-operation and Tax Administration Division at the OECD Centre for Tax Policy and Administration (fta@oecd.org).

Acknowledgements

The study was commissioned by the Forum on Tax Administration (FTA) and co-sponsored by the Commissioner of the Canada Revenue Agency, Mr. Andrew Treusch, and the Commissioner of China's State Administration of Taxation, Mr. Wang Jun. It has been prepared in collaboration with a task team from Australia, Hungary, Ireland, Japan, Spain, Netherlands, New Zealand, United Kingdom and the United States with support from the OECD Secretariat. The project has further benefited from input and feedback from the FTA membership via a survey.

Table of contents

Figures

Tables

Boxes

Acronyms, abbreviations and key definitions

AEOI	Automatic Exchange of Information
ATAF	African Tax Administration Forum
BEPS	Base Erosion and Profit Shifting
CATA	Commonwealth Association of Tax Administrations
CFA	Committee on Fiscal Affairs
CIAT	Inter-American Centre for Tax Administration
CREDAF	Centre de Rencontres et d'Études des Dirigeants des Administrations Fiscales
CRS	Common Reporting Standard
CTPA	Centre for Tax Policy and Administration
DAC	Development Assistance Committee
DRM	Domestic Resource Mobilisation
DWG	Development Working Group
EU	European Union
FTA	Forum on Tax Administration
GRP	Global Relations Programme
IMF	International Monetary Fund
IOTA	Intra-European Organisation of Tax Administrations
ITC	International Tax Compact
KSP	Knowledge Sharing Platform
LTTA	Long-Term Technical Assistance
ODA	Official Development Assistance
RA-FIT	Revenue Administration Fiscal Information Tool
RTO	Regional Tax Organisation
SGATAR	Study Group on Asian Tax Administration and Research
STTA	Short-Term Technical Assistance
TADAT	Tax Administration Diagnostic Assessment Tool
TIWB	Tax Inspectors Without Borders
UNDP	United Nations Development Programme
WBG	World Bank Group

Key definitions

A number of terms are used throughout the report. To promote a common understanding of the report's observations and recommendations, these are briefly defined below:

- **Capacity**: the ability of people, organisations and ultimately society as a whole to manage their affairs successfully.
- **Capacity building (tax administration)**: the broad process whereby tax administrations unleash, strengthen, create, adapt and maintain capacity over time.
- **Donor tax administrations**: tax administrations that provide assistance (i.e. supply-side tax administrations).
- **Host tax administrations**: tax administrations that have requested or are receiving assistance.
- **Technical assistance**: direct support to a tax administration, undertaken to support the resolution of a specific issue or need.
- **Universal guidance**: generic materials developed for common use and broad consumption.
- **Whole-of-government**: an approach that transcends portfolio boundaries to maximise coherence in the policy for, and planning and delivery of, capacity building support, typically involving regular co-ordination between development, revenue and finance officials.

Executive summary

Effective tax systems are a critical building block for increased domestic resource mobilisation which is essential for sustainable development, promoting self-reliance, good governance, growth and stability, with particular relevance to developing countries. At the same time, the move to implementation of the G20 tax priorities, namely Base Erosion and Profit Shifting (BEPS) and Automatic Exchange of Information (AEOI), is triggering a parallel shift towards greater inclusiveness of developing countries in the international tax dialogue to ensure that the global problem of international tax evasion and avoidance can be tackled with a global solution.

As a result, tax co-operation has now reached unprecedented levels. Much work has been, and is being, undertaken by various international stakeholders to assist developing countries in building their tax capacity. Notably, in February 2016, the G20 Finance Ministers and Central Bank Governors welcomed a proposal of developing a tax platform jointly by the IMF, OECD, UN and WBG, and called on them to recommend mechanisms to help ensure effective implementation of technical assistance programmes, including how countries can contribute funding for tax projects and direct technical assistance. The international organisations were invited to report back with recommendations at the next meeting to be held on July 2016 (G20 Communiqué, February 2016).

Tax administration lies at the heart of the tax capacity building process. Sharing practical expertise and building and maintaining relationships between tax administrations are critical for effective co-operation. Although priorities and circumstances vary widely across developing countries, the drive to elevate the collective standard of tax administration is an issue of great importance for the tax administration community. FTA member countries play a significant role in tax administration capacity building. This report sets out how the FTA and its member countries can best organise themselves to contribute to capacity building efforts in a co-ordinated and cost-effective way. Fully aware of and recognising the leading work by the international organisations (IMF, WBG, UNDP and the various OECD initiatives) and regional bodies, this report seeks to complement, not duplicate, ongoing work in capacity building, by offering a view from the tax administration community perspective, both in relation to G20 priorities and more generally.

This study is the outcome of a mapping exercise and a survey of FTA member countries, and has drawn on the insights and expertise of a nine-country task team. Together, these inputs have revealed the following:

- **International co-operation is vital and of strategic importance to tax administrations.** In an increasingly integrated international tax system, engaging those beyond the FTA is mutually beneficial and core to the effectiveness of global tax administration – and it is critical to the consistent implementation of BEPS and AEOI.

- **FTA member countries play a key role in supporting capacity building efforts**, both through their engagement in the international and regional tax organisations and through the provision of bilateral support to developing country tax administrations.
- **How donor tax administrations organise for capacity building influences the achievement of meaningful outcomes and efficiencies.** For donor tax administrations, capacity building strategies that prioritise this kind of support can help focus attention where it is most needed, particularly where whole-of-government approaches are in place to amplify benefits; where core or long-term funding enables tax administrations to deliver assistance in a more structured way, rather than on an ad hoc basis; and where sound diagnostics are used as a basis to systematically plan and evaluate their capacity building activities.
- **The increasing demand for capacity building, and the extent to which it draws on scarce knowledge and skills, compels tax administrations to work smarter in delivering assistance**. In practice, not only does this call for more cohesive and strategic ways of working with other stakeholders to avoid duplication and better identify best practices, but also that innovation be embraced. In this regard, solutions – such as the Knowledge Sharing Platform, a global online tool that enables tax administrations and tax organisations to more broadly and instantaneously share knowledge, expertise and innovative practices with counterparts – can serve as a complementary enabling environment and support tool, both generally and in relation to BEPS and AEOI implementation assistance.
- **The value and application of a common approach to capacity building assistance by donor tax administrations merits further exploration**. The FTA is well positioned to facilitate these deliberations, by drawing on the experiences of its member countries, along with their respective relationships with other developing country administrations and/or institutional stakeholders.

Recommendations

In light of these findings, this report offers four key recommendations to guide the early efforts of the FTA and its member countries.

1. **That the FTA and its members adopt and advance a common Tax Administration Capacity Building Framework.** This report proposes a conceptual framework to assist with both individual and collective identification, planning, sequencing and evaluation of initiatives. Although preliminary, it nevertheless offers a starting point for further deliberations on a model for determining where and how to target and invest resources, not only for tax administrations in their individual capacity but also among the collective community of support providers.
2. **That the FTA and its members help strengthen domestic efforts in capacity building by seeking to apply a "whole-of-government" approach in their jurisdictions**. Recognising the benefits in doing so, countries that have shown leadership in this area have begun integrating tax administration activities to development. Whole-of-government approaches, in which priorities and responses are aligned among a donor country tax administration, development agency and finance department, can facilitate more focused and sustainable efforts in improving tax administration capacity.

3. **That the FTA and its members participate in the development of the Knowledge Sharing Platform.** The Knowledge Sharing Platform prototype has been designed to foster closer co-operation with others and to create efficiencies in sharing expertise to support capacity development, and in its end state, is intended for use by all interested tax administrations. With appetite strong among FTA members for innovation in how knowledge is shared, it follows that the FTA should seek to capitalise on the benefits of leveraging technology. As a key partner, the FTA will participate in the governance of the Knowledge Sharing Platform by joining its "Editorial Board" to help shape the Platform's future development, including its co-ordinated management and curation of content.

4. **That the FTA establishes a Capacity Building Network to connect to the work of others.** A number of initiatives are currently underway and have resulted in unprecedented co-operation among international and regional organisations. While some FTA members are part of these organisations and initiatives, more could be done to connect the FTA and its members to support and complement these efforts, with a view to producing mutual and tangible benefits. At the outset, this Network will:

   a. Lead work to further refine the Capacity Building Framework;

   b. Establish and strengthen partnerships with other organisations and programmes; and

   c. Explore methods that could support better co-ordination with other organisations.

Chapter 1

Introduction

This chapter introduces the objectives of the FTA Capacity Building Project and explains the context, research methodology and purpose and structure of this report.

Context and background

G20 Leaders have acknowledged that a robust and efficient tax system is an important element of global economic resilience. In pursuit of this objective, the G20 called on the Organisation for Economic Cooperation and Development (OECD), the International Monetary Fund (IMF), the United Nations and the World Bank Group to advance an interrelated set of priorities aimed at: countering tax evasion, countering tax avoidance, and supporting effective domestic resource mobilisation. These actions are aimed at ensuring developing economies can fully and effectively participate in, and benefit from, the G20 international tax agenda. In February 2016, G20 Finance Ministers endorsed the inclusive framework proposed by the OECD for the global implementation of Base Erosion and Profit Shifting (BEPS) project.

As a result, tax co-operation has now reached unprecedented levels. Much work has been undertaken by various international stakeholders to assist developing countries in building their tax capacity. Notably, in February 2016, the G20 Finance Ministers also welcomed the proposal by the OECD, the IMF, the UN and the World Bank Group to build on their existing co-operation by establishing a platform for collaboration on tax administration technical assistance programmes.

In March 2015, the FTA Bureau initiated a project on tax capacity building as part of its work programme. The Commissioners of Canada and China initiated and led, with support from the FTA Secretariat and a task team comprised of 9 FTA member countries, a project aimed at developing guidance as to how the FTA and its member countries could best organise themselves to contribute to capacity building efforts in a co-ordinated, cost-effective and sustainable way. This work has well-positioned the FTA to respond to the G20's call to action.

Box 1.1. **G20 tax priorities**

The G20 has acknowledged that a robust and efficient tax system is an important element of global economic resilience, and as such calls on the OECD, IMF, UN and World Bank Group to advance a set of interrelated priorities aimed at:

- countering tax avoidance, specifically base erosion and profit shifting (BEPS), and reforming the international tax system;
- countering tax evasion, in particular through the automatic exchange of information (AEOI); and
- supporting effective domestic resource mobilisation (DRM) to ensure developing economies can fully and effectively participate in, and benefit from, the G20 international tax agenda.

Source: G20, 2015.

Methodology

This report drew on three sources of information: a literature review, a survey of the capacity building landscape, and selected country experiences. The literature review covered a full range of publications from multilateral organisations (see "Bibliographies" at the end of each chapter), focused on recent developments in the capacity building domain, and was supplemented by a high level inventory of current capacity building activities. A survey was distributed to all FTA members to better understand their capacity building context and experiences in this area. Twenty-five countries completed the survey. To broaden the range of experience examined and support the analysis and recommendations, this study also gave special attention to the insights of some FTA members' capacity building experience,[1] which are featured in text boxes.

Purpose and structure of the report

The purpose of this study is to identify how tax administrations can better address the increasing demand for capacity building in developing countries, and is intended to complement, not duplicate, the ongoing work in the broader OECD context as well as in other international and regional organisations, both in relation to G20 priorities and more generally. This includes efforts to offer tax administrations early guidance on how to better position themselves to respond to increasing demands and pressures in the capacity building space. It also sets out a way forward for the FTA to support the efforts of its members in this regard.

The report begins with an overview of the current tax capacity building landscape, highlighting key initiatives and recent developments that have emerged in response to developing country needs. Some current practices in the organisation and delivery of capacity building assistance are introduced together with providing some guidance on how capacity building assistance can be organised at the domestic level. A discussion on leveraging technology to work smarter, mainly by taking advantage of the Knowledge Sharing Platform, is then made, followed by international co-operation in enhancing these efforts. The report finally introduces the Tax Administration Capacity Building Framework before concluding with some key observations and a set of recommendations.

Bibliography

G20 (2015), *Development Working Group Domestic Resource Mobilization: G20 Response to 2014 Reports on Base Erosion and Profit Shifting and Automatic Exchange of Tax Information for Developing Economies 2015*, www.g20australia.org/official_resources/g20_response_2014_reports_base_erosion_and_profit_shifting_and_automatic_exchange.

Note

1. The informal task group comprised of Australia, Canada, China, Hungary, Ireland, Japan, Spain, Netherlands, New Zealand, United Kingdom and the United States.

Chapter 2

Overview of current tax capacity building landscape

This chapter examines the current capacity building landscape through the respective lenses of international priorities, institutional stakeholders, and recent key developments. It then explores the role of donor tax administrations in supporting capacity building efforts.

Effective tax systems are critical for ensuring that developing economies have sustainable sources of government revenue and can help support good governance. At the same time, the shift from policy to implementation of the G20 tax priorities, namely Base Erosion and Profit Shifting (BEPS) and Automatic Exchange of Information (AEOI), is also triggering a parallel shift towards greater inclusiveness of developing countries in the global tax dialogue. These challenges create an increasing demand for tax capacity building for developing countries, and call for multilateral and bilateral initiatives to be best organised to address this demand in a co-ordinated, cost-effective and sustainable way.

The role of capacity building for effective taxation

Tax and non-tax revenue are vital components of domestic resource mobilisation (DRM), aimed at providing governments with independent resources for investing in development, delivering public services, and increasing state capacity, accountability and responsiveness to their citizens. The quality of the tax system – both tax policy and tax administration – is itself a central pillar of state-building and good governance (OECD, 2013:26). This is true for both developed and developing countries. It is notable that developing countries' domestic resources provide by far the largest share of financing for development, even in the poorest countries. In 2012, total tax revenues collected in Africa were 10 times greater than what countries received in the form of official development assistance (ODA).

Box 2.1. **Tax administration capacity building needs**

Priorities and circumstances vary widely across developing countries, but there is considerable commonality in the core challenges they face. Capacity in all areas remains work in progress, and work to improve fundamental operations (e.g. taxpayer education, information management, auditing, and debt collection), remains critical, as well as ensuring stable and empowered management.

Source: IMF Report on *Current Challenges in Revenue Mobilization* (IMF, 2015b).

Raising tax revenue, however, poses many challenges for developing countries. Specific challenges that loom especially large include weak tax administrations, low taxpayer morale and compliance, corruption and poor governance, prevalence of "hard-to-tax" sectors, a small tax base and the missing reciprocal link between tax and public and social expenditures. In addition, many developing countries continue to depend heavily on trade tax revenues, yet trade liberalisation increasingly reduces revenue from tariffs on imports and exports, obliging them to seek other sources from which to generate tax revenue. Striking the right balance between creating an attractive tax regime for domestic and foreign investment (e.g. through lower tax rates on corporate income or through tax expenditures), and securing the necessary revenues for public spending, is another key policy dilemma. Developing countries also face challenges in designing and implementing effective transfer pricing and information exchange regimes, and more generally in improving transparency. Tax capacity building is therefore an absolute precondition for developing countries to mobilise domestic resources for an eventual exit from aid dependency and the accomplishment of the Sustainable Development Goals agreed to in September 2015 through the United Nations process.

BEPS and automatic exchange of information

In the meantime, a globalised economy has put a strain on the international tax framework, revealing weaknesses that create opportunities for BEPS, thus requiring a bold move by policy makers to restore confidence in the system and ensure that profits are taxed where economic activities take place and value is created. In September 2013, G20 Leaders endorsed the ambitious and comprehensive Action Plan on BEPS and in 2015 applauded the timely delivery of the BEPS report package. Importantly, the final package of BEPS measures included new minimum standards on: country-by-country reporting, treaty shopping, curbing harmful tax practices, and, effective mutual agreement procedures.

Box 2.2. **BEPS in the developing country context**

Developing countries face difficulties in building the capacity needed to implement highly complex rules and to challenge well-advised and experienced MNEs. These include:

- competing priorities, often with inadequate staffing;
- uncompetitive compensation for staff working on international tax avoidance issues, leading to a constant drain to the private sector, particularly the large accountancy firms, that when combined with lack of experience, results in a well-known asymmetry when officials are confronted by well-advised large companies; and
- a lack of established practices for settling disputes with large corporations.

Source: OECD (2014b: 33).

Acknowledging that developing countries face specific policy issues and implementation challenges that are not always shared with developed countries, in November 2014 the OECD launched a new strategy for deepening developing countries' engagement in the BEPS Project, with direct participation in the CFA and its technical working groups by more countries and by regional tax organisations as well as the establishment of regional networks and a ramping up of capacity-building support. This engagement includes the development of tools specifically designed for developing countries to address all of the key BEPS concerns they expressed, as well as those not captured by the BEPS Action Plan. This also means that a significant number of developing countries were at the table and actively involved in the crucial decisions on BEPS solutions. Over the next two years, practical and administrable tools will be presented to ensure that developing countries can address their BEPS concerns effectively and efficiently.

International progress is also being made in the fight against tax evasion. In July 2014, the OECD developed and endorsed a proposal for a new single global standard for automatic exchange of information in response to a request by G20 leaders at their summit in September 2013. The standard calls on jurisdictions to obtain information from their financial institutions and automatically exchange that information with other jurisdictions on an annual basis.

Developing countries stand to gain from the implementation of this new global standard in their fight against illicit financial flows, by increasing their revenue collection and deterring tax evasion. G20 governments have mandated the OECD-hosted Global Forum on Transparency and Exchange of Information for Tax Purposes, working with the

OECD Task Force on Tax and Development, to help developing countries identify their needs for technical assistance and capacity building in order to participate in and benefit from automatic exchange of information. In September 2014, the Global Forum presented its roadmap to the G20 spelling out how developing countries can overcome obstacles to participate in the automatic exchange standard and meet its requirements. The roadmap describes a staged approach for how developing countries can participate in the new standard and includes an outline for pilot projects to be undertaken between developing and developed country partners, working with the Global Forum Secretariat, to address awareness and capacity constraints (OECD, 2014a: 172-173).

Need for broader response

As both BEPS and AEOI are moving to implementation, they demand the full participation of tax administrations from developed and developing countries to ensure that the global problem of international tax evasion and avoidance can be tackled with a global solution, and that developing countries can also reap the benefit of the G20's international tax agenda. To this end, the G20 Development Working Group (DWG) agreed to the "G20 Response to 2014 Reports on Base Erosion and Profit Shifting and Automatic Exchange of Tax information for Developing Economies" at its September 2014 Meeting, which was endorsed by G20 Finance Ministers later that month. The response outlines "New Action 3: Strengthen Capacity" as a priority area for the DWG's domestic resource mobilisation work for 2015 and beyond, and acknowledges the essential and inherent role of capacity building, including assistance provided by tax administration experts, to the comprehensive implementation of BEPS and AEOI (G20, 2015b).

Box 2.3. **G20 Development Working Group**

The G20 Development Working Group has developed a guiding framework for responding to capacity issues arising from the G20 tax agenda. Efforts to strengthen developing countries' capacity in tackling BEPS and implementing the new standard for AEOI should:

1. be sequenced with support for other tax priorities, where necessary starting with the building blocks for effective tax systems;
2. target areas of priority identified by partner governments, considered on a case-by-case basis;
3. be co-ordinated within and between providers of development co-operation;
4. include consideration of developing countries' capacity to reap the benefits of reforms; and
5. promote developing countries' participation in the international tax architecture.

Source: G20 Development Working Group guiding framework for responding to capacity issues arising from G20 agenda (G20, 2015b: Annex 4).

This concern was further echoed and addressed by the **Addis Tax Initiative** launched in July 2015 by 30 jurisdictions (including 17 FTA member countries[1]) at the Third International Conference on International Financing for Development in Addis Ababa, Ethiopia, which established a commitment to accelerate international capacity building. To do so, the **Addis Tax Initiative** called for participating providers of international support to collectively double their technical co-operation in the area of domestic revenue mobilisation and taxation by 2020 – a commitment made in anticipation that the need for capacity building support in tax administration and tax policy will outstrip funding availability, and one that was eagerly welcomed by developing country partners with a reciprocal commitment to step up their own efforts to drive forward reforms (The Addis Tax Initiative Declaration, 2015).

Institutional landscape

Various international actors play a key role in tax capacity building support for developing countries. With strong institutional links, multilateral organisations (i.e. international and regional tax organisations) maintain an ongoing dialogue on key tax reform issues with government through a variety of ways.

For instance, the OECD, through its Tax and Development Programme, Global Relations Programme, Tax and Crime Programme, as well as the Global Forum on Transparency and Exchange of Information for Tax Purposes, seeks to improve the enabling environment for developing countries to build up their capacity in collecting tax fairly and efficiently.

Box 2.4. **OECD Global Relations Programme**

The Global Relations Programme is an extensive and integrated global programme that serves as the OECD's primary outreach mechanism between its Committee on Fiscal Affairs (CFA) and non-OECD member countries (including regional tax organisations). The Programme has as a core element an annual series of approximately 75 interactive learning events covering a broad range of tax policy and administration topics that are delivered primarily to participants from non-OECD economies (including developing countries) with the support of FTA member country experts, for a collective annual contribution of over EUR 3 million. Learning events are delivered through an infrastructure of multilateral tax centres which span the globe.

Source: OECD global relations in taxation, www.oecd.org/tax/tax-global.

The IMF provides policy advice to strengthen macroeconomic policies and technical assistance to build state capacity in government agencies (for example, revenue collection, public finance and investment management, and effective spending), and resources to boost economic resilience against adverse shocks. It has also started deepening its focus on strengthening revenue mobilisation in developing countries, and will further enhance its technical assistance efforts in supporting and strengthening nationally-built revenue reform strategies and apply its recently built and tested tools to deliver effective support in building revenue capacity.

The World Bank has a long history in supporting domestic revenue mobilisation (DRM) in developing countries. In response to the Addis Tax Initiative, the WBG has developed a strategic focus and coherent framework to its work on DRM through the Global Tax Programme. The overall purpose of the programme is to support reform by a wide range of instruments, including analytical work, technical assistance, investment and development policy lending. In particular, it can implement a broad package of activities tailored to a country's specific policy and capacity development needs and assist the respective authorities to address key aspects of international tax issues within the context of the Addis Tax Initiative and beyond.

The UNDP positions capacity development as the organisation's overarching service to programme countries, and approaches it with a five-step process cycle, which includes: 1. Engage stakeholders on capacity development; 2. Assess capacity assets and needs; 3. Formulate a capacity development response; 4. Implement a capacity development response; 5. Evaluate capacity development (UNDP, 2008).

The European Union (EU) has provided significant assistance to developing and accession countries, for instance, through EU budget support programmes which funded twinning projects as well as the European Commission's funded EUROSOCIAL programme (focused on Latin America) and Structural Reform Support Service (focused on EU member states).

In the broader landscape of tax administration capacity building, regional tax organisations also play an important role. These organisations, including the Inter-American Centre for Tax Administration (CIAT), the African Tax Administration forum (ATAF), the Centre de rencontres et d'études des dirigeants des administrations fiscales (CREDAF), the Intra-European Organisation of Tax Administrations (IOTA), the Commonwealth Association of Tax Administrations (CATA), and the Study Group on Asian Tax Administration and Research (SGATAR), as well as the BRICS nations (Brazil, Russia, India, China, South Africa), share a common focus on strengthening capacity in member country tax administrations through knowledge sharing and exchange, and, where relevant, serve as leading promoters of south-south co-operation which are sources of information and experience that are an important asset for developing countries.

Finally, taxation is increasingly an area of focus for national development agencies, which typically have scope within their suite of funding mechanisms to invest in bilateral technical assistance work (OECD, 2013).

Nonetheless, until recently, tax as a development issue has been somewhat neglected by much of the international community, despite some high rates of return and evidence of success. Currently, only around 0.1% of official development assistance (ODA) (excluding that provided by the International Monetary Fund) goes to support the development of tax systems in developing countries. The share of aid specific to developing countries tax reform in the total ODA of OECD member countries was only 0.22% in 2012, a figure that had nonetheless risen from around 0.05% in 2006. International support to tax reform has, in the view of many observers and several surveys, been effective. For instance, within the broader area of support to core public sector services, including civil-service and judicial reform, tax reform is among the areas where the World Bank deems its aid to have been most effective (ITC and OECD, 2015: 4).

Recent key developments

Support for G20 priorities

BEPS consultations through G20/OECD processes have revealed capacity building to be one of the biggest challenges faced by developing countries. Not only does this impact their ability to address BEPS issues generally, but moreover, gaps in capacity, along with a lack of effective legislation, may present opportunities for simpler, but potentially more aggressive tax avoidance than is typically encountered in developed economies (OECD, 2014b: 33).

In view of the need for concrete support to assist developing countries implement BEPS action items, in 2014 the G20 mandated the development of eight practical toolkits to be delivered over the 2016-2018 period by the OECD in co-operation with other international and regional tax organisations (OECD, 2015b). These toolkits are intended to contain reports, guidance, model legislation, train the trainers materials and other tools to facilitate the work of tax administrations.

Box 2.5. **BEPS Toolkits for Developing Countries**

1. Report on tax incentives
2. Tools on lack of comparables for transfer pricing purposes
3. Report on indirect transfers of assets
4. Toolkit on transfer pricing documentation requirements
5. Toolkit on tax treaty negotiation
6. Toolkit on base eroding payments
7. Toolkit on supply chain restructuring
8. Toolkit on assessment of BEPS risks

Source: OECD (2014c).

Additionally, in 2015, regional networks were established to facilitate an ongoing and more structured dialogue process on BEPS with a broader group of developing countries, particularly low-income countries, with the participation of regional tax organisations where relevant.

At the third meeting of BRICS' Heads of Tax Authorities, held in Moscow in November 2015, commissioners agreed that it is in the common interest for both developed countries and developing countries to combat international tax avoidance, and furthermore, that developing countries who are interested should be involved and be provided with technical assistance in the implementation of BEPS actions.

Engagement of developing countries on BEPS (and on the international tax agenda in general) is a welcomed and encouraged practice as it is essential to ensuring that they receive appropriate support for the challenges they face. Further, the OECD has since developed an inclusive framework for the global implementation of the BEPS project, which was endorsed by G20 Finance Ministers at their February 2016 meeting. This approach will see all interested and committed jurisdictions participating on an equal footing to review the implementation of the BEPS minimum standards, as well as monitor the package as a whole and complete the remaining elements of the BEPS standard-setting work. Importantly, the framework recognises the important role that tax administrations – and the FTA – will have in supporting the implementation process.

Likewise, in 2014 the G20 asked the Global Forum, working with the World Bank Group and other organisations, to facilitate pilot projects to assist developing countries to implement the new standard on automatic exchange of financial account information for tax purposes. With the assistance of G20 countries, several pilot projects began in 2015.

It is also notable that in 2015 the G20 Development Working Group called on members to "increase peer-to-peer efforts to meet individual targets for support to developing country tax administration capacity building". Further, with momentum around tax co-operation continuing to build in the context of the G20 agenda, international organisations – specifically the OECD, the UN, the IMF and the World Bank – agreed in early 2016 to establish a "platform for collaboration on tax" to deliver joint outputs and support work on tax issues in their respective member countries (OECD, 2016).

Box 2.6. **Spain's AEOI pilot with Colombia**

In the context of its membership in the Global Forum on Transparency and Exchange of Information, Spain is supporting Colombia's implementation of the Common Reporting Standard (CRS) for the automatic exchange of information (AEOI). The project – the first of several pilots, and the most advanced – makes use of peer-to-peer knowledge transfers while employing a step-by-step approach to implementation, having as an objective that Colombia implement and benefit from AEOI in a timely manner. Spain's leadership in promoting the CRS, and its significant experience with automatic exchange of information, were key factors in its decision to enter into this pilot partnership project with Colombia.

The pilot project considers three main components that together underpin successful implementation. Spain and Colombia, with support from the Global Forum and the World Bank Group, have worked on these components, which encompass the need for:

- an adequate legal framework (i.e. the legislation needed to develop to implement CRS, including that which imposes a reporting obligation on financial institutions);
- administrative capacity (i.e. human resources and information technology infrastructure); and
- confidentiality and data safeguards (i.e. adequate rules and procedures).

Source: Spanish Tax Agency.

Tax Inspectors Without Borders

Established first as a feasibility study in 2013 under the auspices of the OECD Tax and Development Programme, the Tax Inspectors Without Borders (TIWB) initiative was officially launched as a partnership between the OECD and the United Nations Development Programme (UNDP) in 2015 during the Third International Conference on Financing for Development as a means to support developing countries build tax audit capacity in view of broader DRM objectives. TIWB enables the transfer of tax audit knowledge and skills

Box 2.7. **Netherlands' TIWB experience: Ghana Project**

The first TIWB pilot programme was set up between Ghana (GRA) and the Netherlands (NTCA). The scope of the programme was to work jointly on tax audit and audit related issues regarding transfer pricing, such as risk assessment and case selection. Dutch experts have worked in Ghana together with and alongside their GRA counterparts on actual cases. Although the pilot phase of the programme was temporarily put on hold by unforeseen circumstances (the Ebola crisis), upon its resumption, the programme continued with good results and concrete outcomes. Procedures on risk assessment and case selection were improved and the tax audit approach on TP-related aspects was developed further. After a two year period, the pilot phase concluded. Both the GRA and the NTCA consider the outcomes and concrete results achieved thus far to be positive, and supported the project's continuation as a regular TWIB programme. The pilot phase also demonstrated that the TIWB concept in its pure form (and as described in the TIWB Toolkit) has added value as a niche area in technical assistance. The GRA and the NTCA will therefore continue their joint efforts on TIWB under a regular TIWB-programme for the coming years.

Source: Tax and Customs Administration, Netherlands.

to tax administrations in developing countries through a real time, "learning by doing" approach. This knowledge and skill transfer is accomplished through the deployment of experts (currently serving or recently retired tax officials) who work directly with local tax officials on current audits and audit-related issues concerning international tax matters. A number of pilot projects and international tax workshops are already underway.

Tax Administration Diagnostic Assessment Tool

In 2015, the IMF and several international partners (European Commission, the IMF, Germany, Japan, Netherlands, Norway, Switzerland, United Kingdom and the World Bank) released the Tax Administration Diagnostic Assessment Tool (TADAT). TADAT is available for use by country authorities and those assisting them.

TADAT is designed to provide an objective and consistent assessment of the health of key components of a country's system of tax administration. It works by evaluating a tax administration in each of nine performance outcome areas:

- the integrity of the registered taxpayer base;
- the extent of understanding about the compliance risks in the tax system;
- the quality of support provided to taxpayers to promote voluntary compliance;
- the extent to which taxpayers meet their filing obligations;
- the extent to which taxpayers meet their payment obligations;
- the accuracy with which taxpayers declare their tax obligations;
- the adequacy of tax dispute resolution;
- the efficiency of tax administration; and
- the level of accountability and transparency.

Assessment results can then be used to identify the relative strengths and weaknesses in a tax administration's systems, processes, and institution. TADAT also provides a basis for monitoring and evaluating reform progress towards established targets, through repeat assessments.

Notably, the 2015 Addis Tax Initiative Declaration highlighted TADAT as a helpful development in view of the broader benefits that diagnostic assessments of country tax systems can bring to bear in terms of determining where capacity building will be most effective (The Addis Tax Initiative Declaration, 2015).

Revenue Administration Fiscal Information Tool

In 2012, the IMF developed the web-based Revenue Administration Fiscal Information Tool (RA-FIT) to generate a standardised set of data from and for all customs and taxation administrations on a regular basis, allowing them to monitor basic aspects of their performance more effectively and compare themselves against peers while at the same time enabling better technical assistance work by having data in advance of planned activities. To date, RA-FIT has been used in two instances: first in 2012 to gather information from more than 80 developing countries, and subsequently in 2014 by the same group with additional input from up to 38 members of CIAT. Additionally in 2014, the OECD signed a Letter of Intent with the IMF, IOTA and CIAT to jointly use the RA-FIT platform to collect and share data and information from their respective members tax administrations on a common set of data elements.

Tax and Development Transfer Pricing Assistance Programme

In 2011, the OECD's Task Force on Tax and Development, in partnership with the European Commission and World Bank Group, began a programme of support for developing countries seeking to implement or strengthen their transfer pricing rules. To date, country-specific support initiatives have been put in place in sixteen jurisdictions, and a regional project is also underway in West Africa.

Box 2.8. **Selected Transfer Pricing Assistance Programme results**

- In Colombia, revenues increased ten-fold from USD 3.3 mln in 2011 to over USD 33 mln in 2014 from transfer pricing adjustments made as a result of audits of multinational enterprises.
- In Vietnam, the number of audits conducted by the tax administration increased from 1 audit in 2012 to 40 audits in 2013, giving rise to transfer pricing adjustments of USD 110 mln by the end of 2013.
- In Zambia, revenue from audits has increased from USD 3.22 mln in 2012 to USD 7.91 mln in 2013.
- In Kenya, revenue collection from transfer pricing audits has doubled from USD 52 mln in 2012 to USD 107 mln in 2014.

Source: Developing Capacity in Transfer Pricing, OECD (2015c).

This programme has had a significant impact in many countries through the introduction of transfer pricing rules aligned with international standards and the establishment of specialist units to carry out the transfer pricing work. Revenue from transfer pricing audits has also increased. Importantly, this work is closely aligned with existing country tax reform programmes and establishes the foundation for other support or activities, such as the TIWB initiative, to further expand the impact of the programme.

Task Force on Tax and Development

The OECD Task Force on Tax and Development, co-chaired by senior representatives of the Governments of South Africa and the Netherlands, brings together stakeholders to discuss current tax and development issues facing developing countries. Its role is to advise the OECD's Committee on Fiscal Affairs (CFA) and the Development Assistance Committee (DAC) in delivering its Tax and Development Programme. Since its creation in 2010, its members meet annually to monitor progress and identify areas of opportunity for working with developing countries. The Task Force most recently met in November 2015, where it recognised (among other issues) "the need to invest in building expertise in the developing world to build local capacity to address tax evasion and avoidance concerns" and reaffirmed "the importance for international and regional organisations, donors, the private sector and business to work coherently to deliver assistance to avoid duplication and fragmented initiatives" (OECD, 2015b).

Role of tax administrations

Tax administration lies at the heart of the tax capacity building process. Sharing practical expertise and building and maintaining relationships between tax administrations are critical for effective co-operation. It is perhaps unsurprising then that for the tax administration community, the drive to elevate the collective standard of tax administration is an issue of great importance.

As discussed above, ensuring that developing countries can reap the full benefits of international tax reforms has important implications, not only in terms of DRM but also in terms of the integrity of the reforms themselves; without consistent application of tools and methods, the effectiveness of any new measure is unlikely to reach its full potential. As key donor tax administrations, FTA member countries play a key role in supporting capacity building efforts, both via their engagement in the international and regional tax organisations and as part of bilateral support to developing country tax administrations. For instance, a recent study (G20, 2015b: Annex 3) of the tax-related development co-operation efforts undertaken by G20 members confirmed that support is indeed being provided, and moreover, noted that:

- to the extent reported, assistance has largely targeted low and lower-middle income countries;
- despite broad geographic distribution of activities overall, there are pockets of concentrated activities, raising the likelihood of multiple G20 members undertaking bilateral tax-related development co-operation with a given recipient country;
- the focus of G20 assistance tends to be on matters of domestic taxation (i.e. core building blocks) rather than international taxation – although this does not come at the complete exclusion of working relationships with international or regional tax organisations which tend to focus efforts on international taxation matters; and
- the vast majority of activity appears to be undertaken in the form of bilateral, regional or multilateral initiatives funded through official development assistance (ODA) mechanisms, with technical assistance activities being among the most common – perhaps explaining in part the emphasis on the core building blocks of taxation.

Box 2.9. **Italy's engagement with Albania**

Italy is working with Albania to improve tax administration capacity on multiple fronts. In the context of their mutual membership in the Global Forum for Transparency and Exchange of Information, Italy has partnered with Albania to implement an AEOI pilot project. In particular, Italy will offer assistance on four dimensions of CRS implementation: regulatory provisions; data security and protection; information technology and informatics support; and, information exchange. The Italian contribution to the pilot project will be in the form of supporting technical implementation of CRS, consulting and training Albanian tax officials (classes and on-the-job) to allow the Albanian Government to make the first automatic exchange of information according to the CRS by the end of September 2018. Italy and Albania will continue their joint efforts on AEOI pilot project for the coming years.

Separately under the auspices of the TIWB initiative, the Agenzia delle Entrate (AdE) has also concluded in 2015 a co-operation agreement with Albania for the deployment of an Italian transfer pricing expert to the Albanian Tax Administration (ATD) for a one year period carrying out a "learning by doing" approach in dealing with complex international tax matters. The project was divided in two stages: the first one devoted to risk assessment analysis; and, the second to audits of taxpayers analysed in the first phase, and enhancing and promoting taxpayer compliance with the aim to understand the taxpayer's business. Both AdE an ATD consider the outcome and concrete results of TIWB project achieved. The successful outcome of the project is the result of the commitment of the TIWB working group composed of Italian and Albanian tax officials.

Source: Agenzia delle Entrate, Italy.

Separate OECD work has found that technical assistance is a central element in virtually every aid programme on taxation and that many host country tax officials favour assistance that takes the form of experts who work long-term "in the trenches" to serve as mentors and respond to changing needs (OECD, 2013).

However, amid the full range of capacity building initiatives and commitments, donor tax administrations are confronting growing demand for expertise that is increasingly difficult to match, with further increases anticipated with the implementation of BEPS and AEOI.

Box 2.10. **Developing countries and BEPS**

Capacity building to address BEPS issues has been identified as key cross cutting challenges for developing countries, particularly as the implementation of the BEPS measures begins. However, it is also important to be aware that although the implementation of the G20 tax agenda sets extra demands for capacity building, developing countries still have increasing expectations in broader tax implementation topics such as how to achieve higher levels of tax compliance and prevent tax fraud, and how to build capacity for improving cross-border taxation.

Source: Developing countries and BEPS, www.oecd.org/tax/developing-countries-and-beps.htm.

Note

1. The 17 countries are: Australia, Belgium, Canada, Denmark, Finland, France, Germany, Indonesia, Italy, Korea, Luxembourg, Netherlands, Norway, Slovenia, Sweden, United Kingdom and United States.

Bibliography

Addis Tax Initiative Declaration (2015), *Third International Conference on Financing for Development*, Addis Ababa, www.taxcompact.net/documents/Addis-Tax-Initiative_Declaration.pdf.

G20 (2015a), *Development Working Group Domestic Resource Mobilisation: Call to Action for Strengthening Tax Capacity in Developing Countries*, www.g20.org/English/Documents/PastPresidency/201512/P020151228308622272822.pdf.

G20 (2015b), *Development Working Group Domestic Resource Mobilization: G20 Response to 2014 Reports on Base Erosion and Profit Shifting and Automatic Exchange of Tax Information for Developing Economies 2015,* www.g20australia.org/official_resources/g20_response_2014_reports_base_erosion_and_profit_shifting_and_automatic_exchange.

IMF, OECD, UN and World Bank (2011), *Supporting the Development of More Effective Tax Systems – A Report to the G20 Development Working Group.*

IMF (2015a), *The Role of the IMF in Supporting the Implementation of the Post-2015 Development Agenda*, http://siteresources.worldbank.org/DEVCOMMINT/Documentation/23689846/DC2015-0005(E)RoleofIMF.pdf, https://www.imf.org/external/np/g20/pdf/11031.pdf.

IMF (2015b), *Current Challenges in Revenue Mobilization: Improving Tax Compliance*, www.imf.org/external/np/pp/eng/2015/020215a.pdf.

ITC and OECD (2015), *Examples of Successful DRM Reforms and the Role of International Co-operation*, Discussion Paper, www.oecd.org/ctp/tax-global/examples-of-successful-DRM-reforms-and-the-role-of-international-co-operation.pdf, Deutsche Gesellschaft für, Bonn.

OECD (2016), *Secretary General Report to G20 Finance Ministers*, Paris, 26 February. www.oecd.org/g20/topics/taxation/oecd-secretary-general-tax-report-g20-finance-ministers-february-2016.PDF.

OECD (2015a), Centre for Tax Policy and Administration, *Global Relations Tax Programme 2015 Annual Report*, Paris, www.oecd.org/ctp/tax-global/Global-Relations-Tax-Programme-Annual-Report.pdf.

OECD (2015b), *Co-Chair Statement on the Meeting of the OECD Task Force on Tax and Development*, Paris, November 2015, www.oecd.org/tax/tax-global/fifth-task-force-tax-development-co-chair-statement.pdf.

OECD (2015c), *Developing Capacity in Transfer Pricing*, www.oecd.org/tax/tax-global/developing-capacity-in-transfer-pricing-flyer.pdf.

OECD (2014a), *Development Co-operation Report 2014: Mobilising Resources for Sustainable Development*, OECD Publishing, Paris, http://dx.doi.org/10.1787/dcr-2014-en.

OECD (2014b), *Part 1 of a Report to G20 Development Working Group on The Impact of BEPS in Low Income Countries*, OECD Publishing, Paris.

OECD (2014c), *Addressing developing countries' international tax concerns* www.oecd.org/ctp/addressing-developing-countries-international-tax-concerns.htm.

OECD (2013), *Tax and Development, Aid Modalities for Strengthening Tax Systems,* OECD Publishing, Paris, http://dx.doi.org/10.1787/9789264177581-en.

The World Bank: *Capacity Development in Practice*, http://web.worldbank.org/WBSITE/EXTERNAL/TOPICS/EXTCDRC/0,,contentMDK:20273839~menuPK:64169185~pagePK:64169212~piPK:64169110~theSitePK:489952,00.html.

UNDP (2008), *Capacity Development Practice Note*, www.unpcdc.org/media/8651/pn_capacity_development.pdf.

UNDP (2009), *Capacity Development: A UNDP Primer*, www.undp.org/content/dam/aplaws/publication/en/publications/capacity-development/capacity-development-a-undp-primer/CDG_PrimerReport_final_web.pdf.

Chapter 3

Domestic organisation of capacity building assistance

This chapter explores how domestic resources can be better mobilised to deliver capacity building support by exploring donor tax administration practices with regards to strategies, programme development, delivery approach, resourcing and evaluation.

The support that tax administrations provide to developing countries is one important way in which individual governments and the international community can support tax capacity building in developing countries. Though capacity building and providing technical assistance are increasingly important for many donor countries, the capacity of donor country tax administrations to engage in such activities is limited. As noted in the OECD publication, *Tax Administration 2015* (OECD, 2015), many tax administrations have been subject to fiscal consolidation efforts in recent years, and so in many cases, efforts are constrained by budget and resource availability. Moreover, for donor tax administrations that must also deliver on domestic mandates, capacity building commitments and demands must be balanced against operational requirements and pressures. This includes the need for donor tax administrations to deliver on their own outcomes for BEPS and AEOI implementation, a circumstance which is only likely to amplify competing claims on expert resources. A key challenge therefore is how to reconcile these demands.

Demands and commitments in this area are increasingly creating important pressures on tax administration resources. This implies that efforts need to be carefully managed in order to deliver results and to do so in an efficient way. Having a structured, comprehensive and sustainable approach therefore holds the potential to help tax administrations better manage demand without compromising responsiveness. To this end, this Chapter explores donor tax administration practices with regards to strategies, programme development, delivery approach, resourcing and evaluation.

Strategies

Strategic planning, as a basis for setting goals and effectively managing resources, is well established for FTA tax administrations (OECD, 2015). Typically, these plans focus on a tax administration's core business programmes, for example, as they relate to compliance or service. However, little effort appears to have been invested in the development of capacity building strategies. The absence of a clearly articulated strategy may imply that activities are determined on an ad-hoc basis, with resources being misaligned with priorities or spread too thin, and where the collective outcomes of activities do not surpass the value of investments in them.

Fundamentally, the provision of capacity building support is a responsive undertaking. The responsibility for articulating capacity building needs, whether policy or administrative, rests with the host government. This principle is well-established with regards to mobilising domestic resources for development where best practice calls on international assistance providers to operate according to the Paris Declaration commitments of ownership and alignment, and follow the lead of partner country governments. That said, capacity building also is a practical exercise built on partnerships and mutual interest. That support targets the areas of most need and where improvements in capacity have greatest relative value, is a relevant goal, not only for recipients who are seeking to improve outcomes, but also to providers who are investing scarce resources. Experience suggests that FTA member countries who undertake their capacity building activities in a more strategic manner are better equipped to deliver support. Examples include Japan, Spain, and Sweden, where technical assistance assignments are typically part of the strategic development plans of institutional donor agencies; for instance, the national development agency in the cases of Japan and Sweden, or the European Commission's EUROsociAL Programme in the case of Spain.

Box 3.1. Spain and the EUROsociAL Programme

Spain's Agencia Estatal de Administracion Tributaria (AEAT) acts as one of the operative partners of the European Commission's EUROSOCIAL Programme, which has as its focus strengthening the institutional capacity of public administrations in Latin American countries. This focus aligns well with AEAT's prioritisation of collaboration with Latin-American countries, in view of historical and linguistic ties. In 2015, under the auspices of this Programme, AEAT has carried out several technical assistances missions with several Latin American countries, specifically: Colombia, Costa Rica, México, El Salvador, Brazil and Chile. Notably, for all EUROSOCIAL projects, a post-event report is always required.

Source: Spanish Tax Agency.

Likewise, the Australian Taxation Office and New Zealand's Inland Revenue Department each have a role within their government's strategic assistance plans to improve tax administration capability within the Asia Pacific region, with some activities funded as a result. In the United Kingdom, HM Revenue and Customs' active involvement in tax capacity building efforts is one part of a wider government commitment to support tax reform in developing countries. It is suggested, therefore, that donor tax administrations develop a strategy before investing significant resources in capacity building activities. An effective capacity building strategy may need to take the following elements into account:

- the goals and priorities of the donor government;
- the capability, or expertise, of the donor tax administration;
- resourcing and funding;
- preferred delivery mechanisms; and
- evaluation of the impacts and results.

Box 3.2. Taking a "whole of government" approach to maximise policy coherence and aid effectiveness

"... This 'whole-of-government' approach should involve regular co-ordination between development, revenue and finance officials to maximise policy coherence. The various ministries can co-ordinate efforts on a broad range of issues, from helping to deliver technical assistance for capacity building in developing countries (in revenue authorities and tax policy for example) through to understanding how development policy objectives can be achieved through non-classical policy levers...

Donor agencies should avoid taking a supply-driven approach and respond with a flexible and complementary mix of short- and longer-term support."

Source: Principles For International Engagement In Supporting Developing Countries In Revenue Matters (OECD, 2013).

In developing a strategy, donor tax administrations are encouraged to discuss goals and priorities with other domestic government partners, namely foreign affairs, treasury, and international development, to ensure that efforts are aligned with the government's overall goals and priorities and to set the stage for (potential) whole-of-government approaches that co-ordinate or integrate specific efforts. Engagement with domestic government partners at the earliest appropriate juncture can help determine whether pursuing a whole-of-government approach would be relevant and beneficial, and if so, how this could materialise in practice (e.g. through co-ordinated planning, integrated funding, etc.). Horizontal by nature, this type of approach is designed to transcend portfolio boundaries, and so can have an amplifying effect on long-term outcomes. The OECD, through its Tax and Development Programme, has already established the application of whole-of-government approaches as one of ten key principles for effective delivery of support to developing countries in revenue matters, noting that, "countries providing international assistance have a responsibility to work internally to ensure a coherent and co-ordinated approach" (OECD, 2013). The Addis Declaration embeds this principle by noting in the Declaration that "participants that are OECD members commit to adhere to the OECD *Principles for International Engagement in Supporting Partner Countries in Revenue Matters* (The Addis Tax Initiative Declaration, 2015). This is no less relevant for the delivery of specific support for the implementation of BEPS and AEOI, for which tax administrations have an inherent and critical role, than for capacity building in general.

Box 3.3. "The Belt and Road" Initiative and China SAT's Delivery Efforts

To promote regional economic co-operation, strengthen exchanges and facilitate mutual learning between different jurisdictions, China is conducting a development initiative called "the Belt and Road". Responding positively to this initiative, SAT implemented a series of tax-related measures to improve regional tax administration capacity through co-operation. These include:

- an expanded tax treaty network in line with "The Belt and Road". Countries like Cambodia, Russia, Indonesia, India, Pakistan and Romania either renewed or signed their tax treaties with SAT in 2015.
- the carrying out of extensive research on the tax systems of 95 jurisdictions covering all the countries along "the Belt and Road". Some key outcomes of this research include three Investment Guidelines on Tax Issues with respect to the United States, Mongolia and China Hong Kong.
- providing technical training courses, with the theme of "Collection, Administration and Service" to tax officials from developing countries along "the Belt and Road" including Mongolia, Iraq, Sri Lanka, Bhutan, Moldova and Egypt.

* "The Belt and Road" refers to the Silk Road Economic Belt and 21st-Century Maritime Silk Road. This is a development initiative that aims at instilling vigour and vitality into the ancient Silk Road, to connect Asian, European and African countries more closely and to promote mutually beneficial co-operation.

Source: China State Administration of Taxation.

The merits of greater domestic collaboration have started to be acknowledged by a number of FTA member countries. For example, in 2011 Norway established a Tax for Development programme under its Ministry of Foreign Affairs (as part of the Norwegian Agency for Development Co-operation) to co-ordinate and ensure the quality of Norway's work in areas related to taxation, capital flight and development. In Australia, work is underway to develop a tax and development framework that brings together its foreign aid programme and tax administration activities. In Japan, strong collaboration between the National Tax Agency and the Japan International Co-operation Agency is underpinned by a national framework for technical assistance.

Box 3.4. **Australia's Tax and Development Framework**

While tax administrations are at the heart of tax capacity development to deliver effective tax and development programmes, they must collaborate with other government agencies involved in capability development. The Australian Taxation Office (ATO) works very closely with Australia's lead agency for foreign aid policy and delivery, the Department of Foreign Affairs and Trade (DFAT). Australia has developed a framework for supporting tax policy and administration through aid programmes which aim to guide Australia's approach to assisting partner governments achieve their tax policy and administration goals. The ATO recognises that effective international engagement is the key to building integrity in the global taxation system and it is essential that administrative approaches are achievable in a developing country context. Through this engagement the ATO aims to:

1. be able to better identify and mitigate global risks such as Base Erosion and Profit Shifting,
2. champion international transparency and equitable tax administration,
3. increase collaboration amongst tax administrations, and
4. deliver on Australia's commitment to supporting regional development.

To deliver on these goals the ATO has a range of activities integrated into a cohesive capability development programme. The programme utilises the appropriate and timely elements of other ongoing programmes to deliver capability development activities addressing identified needs, eliminating duplication where possible and focusing on practical outcomes. Approaches used by the ATO include: providing trainers to deliver at selected Global Relations Programmes based on location and topic; development of partnerships with tax administrations of developing countries; active involvement in Australia's regional tax administration group SGATAR (Study Group on Asian Tax Administration and Research); and genuine consideration of capability development requirements when delegates represent the ATO or provide input to the various OECD groups, G20 and other global and regional forums.

Creating strong partnerships with key developing countries by the ATO is done through specific bilateral development programmes using a variety of delivery models including using ATO officers as advisors and mentors on long and short term postings, medium term secondments in and out of the ATO, a visitors programme of short study visits and establishing informal relationships between subject matter experts.

The ATO plans to move capability development approaches towards more collaborative activities, such as joint projects using AEOI data, where development activities can be undertaken as a form of "learning whilst doing", which is expected to also generate revenue results in the shorter term compared to traditional technical training models.

Source: Australian Taxation Office.

Box 3.5. **Japan: Relationship with the Development Agency for the Implementation of Technical Co-operation**

Japan's National Tax Agency (NTA) provides technical co-operation on taxation system and tax administration to developing countries in collaboration with Japan International Co-operation Agency (JICA)*.

As for the procedure of technical co-operation, the process commences with the submission of requests by recipient countries. Following the recipient countries' requests, NTA and JICA identify needs of recipient countries and consider how they could provide technical co-operation for human resources development, organisational strengthening, policy formulation, and institutional development in recipient countries. After their decision to implement technical co-operation, JICA is responsible for overall analysis of the issue, customised multi-year planning (average three years) with due consideration of PDCA, logistic procedures and funding whereas NTA delivers actual technical co-operation with its maximum know-how and expertise. At the end of project term, each project of technical co-operation is evaluated by the evaluation team which consists of both JICA and NTA officials. Whereas JICA evaluates a project in terms of development policy and methodology, NTA does especially from a technical perspective on taxation.

In order to implement projects smoothly throughout the process (from identifying needs to evaluation), NTA dispatches its officials to certain recipient countries as JICA's long-term experts (average three years). They are currently in Cambodia, Indonesia and Vietnam and play important roles as a key co-ordinator among JICA, NTA and tax administration in each recipient country.

*JICA provides development assistance to 154 countries/regions through a variety of schemes such as technical co-operation, loans, and grant aid with the network of about 90 local offices around the world.

Source: Japan's National Tax Agency.

Likewise, donor tax administrations need to consider how and where their respective capabilities and expertise can be best used to reach strategic outcomes. For example, a tax administration that administers a source taxation regime is likely best-positioned to meet requests for assistance on related issues. Consideration also could be given to the scale and modality of assistance in view of funding or resource availability. Some targeting is often required in this regard, so establishing what is feasible should feature within the strategy. Language compatibility, while a practical consideration, is also an important one as it is fundamental to the effective exchange of knowledge and expertise.

Together, these considerations establish the criteria against which individual requests for assistance can be assessed. That is, requests that fit well within the parameters of the strategy deserve consideration, whereas those that do not are likely best directed elsewhere, to be taken up by others.

Programme development

A decision to invest efforts in capacity building should trigger a subsequent – and consultative – programme development process. Reaching a common understanding of, and agreement on, a number of practical matters (e.g. goals, duration, resourcing, etc.) is essential to the smooth and sustainable operation of an assistance effort, particularly in the case of longer-term or ongoing bilateral work. In this regard, a diagnostic of needs is an essential element of the programme development process, as it frames the scoping of activities and offers a warranty against any mismatches between supply and demand. TADAT, described in Chapter 2, offers an example of how an assessment can be undertaken:

- A set of 28 high-level indicators critical to tax administration performance (e.g. on-time filing rate, timeliness of payments) are linked to the nine TADAT performance outcome areas. It is these indicators that are scored and reported upon. A total of 47 measurement dimensions are taken into account in arriving at the indicator scores.
- There are four stages to a TADAT assessment: initiation, based on a formal request from country authorities; pre-assessment, which involves planning and preparation; in-country assessment, to gather information and evidence in respect of each indicator and measurement dimension for scoring purposes; and, post-assessment to finalise the assessment results and report.
- Assessments are conducted by an assessment team typically comprising three or four trained assessors, and can take several weeks to complete (TADAT Field Guide, 2015).

Developing countries differ in their technical capacity (ITC and OECD, 2015) so the practical use and application of assistance received may be a prominent issue for some. Challenges can arise when what has been provided is not exactly what is needed, or when a recipient administrations' readiness to implement is overestimated. In this regard, less targeted efforts may lead to a gap between demand and supply of assistance. To mitigate this risk, donor tax administrations should establish the objective and scope of their capacity building support within the context of diagnostic assessment outcomes. This can be followed by the development of one or more workable plans to guide implementation and ensure effective governance. Often donor tax administrations will want to develop yearly work programmes as a means to prioritise competing demands and assess the implications for resourcing and funding. Carefully scoped programme plans and yearly working plans are the basis for effective governance of tax administrations' efforts. Equally important are appropriate mechanisms for decision-making and strong governance and oversight that bring clarity to partners' respective authorities and accountabilities.

Delivery approach

The delivery of assistance by tax administrations occurs almost exclusively as peer-to-peer exchanges, whereby knowledge and expertise is shared and transferred between tax administration officials. Although there is considerable variety in how peer-to-peer exchanges can occur, the range of activities nevertheless seem to coalesce most commonly in the following ways:

- collaborative exchanges – for instance, for the sharing of best practices – which appear just as likely to occur in a multilateral setting (e.g. conferences) as a bilateral one (e.g. study visits);
- structured learning and training, offered either through multilateral organisations (e.g. OECD Global Relations Programme or regional tax organisations) or on a bilateral basis as part of international co-operation agreements; and
- expert deployments, that is, in-person missions whether they be short or long term. Although these arrangements have tended to occur under the auspices of bilateral co-operation agreements, new initiatives such as the OECD/UN Tax Inspectors Without Borders initiative are bringing a multilateral dimension to how this type of support can be organised.

Box 3.6. **Irish Revenue's co-operation with the Revenue Authority of Rwanda**

Irish Revenue signed a memorandum of co-operation with the Revenue Authority of Rwanda in 2008. This was a bilateral arrangement designed to facilitate the exchange of information and best practice on tax and customs modernisation and specific areas of expertise. It was a joint initiative of the Irish and Rwandan tax administrations.

Under this initiative, Irish Revenue shared its expertise and assisted the Rwanda tax administration to develop and modernise its revenue systems, particularly in relation to the automation of risk assessment systems. The project was funded by Irish Aid, which is part of the Irish Department of Foreign Affairs and Trade. The project involved a number of technical assistance missions to Rwanda, the hosting of study visits in Ireland and the short term secondment of experts.

Source: Irish Revenue.

Although the scope of this project did not allow for a detailed accounting of tax administration activity, it nonetheless appears that on the balance, FTA members show considerable flexibility in how they provide assistance. Specifically, research undertaken for this project shows that:

- work being carried out as structured and long-term bilateral engagement on domestic tax matters is often taking place within the context of broader government development policy;
- activities tend to be undertaken largely, but not exclusively, in FTA members' own or neighbouring regions, with some exceptions where historical or other relationships underpin the capacity building partnership;
- many also have deep multilateral ties beyond the FTA, firstly being engaged (as members) in the work of regional tax organisations which allows for multilateral peer exchanges, including contributions to regional tax organisation initiatives, and secondly, through the substantial participation of FTA tax administrations in the OECD Global Relations Programme, where tax administration officials serve as subject matter experts for the Programme's learning events.

Box 3.7. **Japan's comprehensive delivery approach**

Japan has been providing comprehensive technical co-operation to developing counties. It covers all phases of capacity building from sharing knowledge and best practices, to diagnosing the capacity of recipient countries and to peer to peer dispatch of tax administration officials.

Japan's National Tax Agency (NTA) actively provides bilateral and multilateral technical co-operation to developing countries, focusing on Asian countries, as part of the Japan International Co-operation Agency (JICA) framework (please refer to Box 3.5). This includes the dispatch of NTA officials to recipient countries as JICA's long-term experts to provide continuous advice across the wide range of tax administration matters, as well as the provision of training courses on international taxation and the Japanese tax administration system. Funding for these projects is provided by JICA.

Box 3.7. **Japan's comprehensive delivery approach** *(continued)*

The Japanese government contributes to the implementation of the Asian Development Bank's technical assistance project which aims to support the capacity development of tax authorities in developing countries which include those participating in SGATAR through the Japan Fund For Poverty Reduction established in the Asian Development Bank. As for contributions in personnel, the Japanese government provides its officials as experts to workshops held as part of the project as well as dispatch of its officials to the Asian Development Bank to manage the project.

The Japanese government also has been supporting the OECD's Global Relations Programme for more than 20 years not only by providing its officials to the seminars for developing countries in practice to share knowledge and best practices but through financial contributions as well as dispatch of its officials to OECD to assist the management of the project.

The Japanese government also has been making contributions by funding technical assistance programmes of IMF to build strong governmental institutions. As to the TADAT programme, NTA provides funding and dispatches an assessor for its implementation. The Japanese government has recently decided to make a substantial contribution to the Revenue Mobilisation Trust Fund (RMTF) of the IMF to effectively enhance the capacity on taxation in developing counties.

Finally, when implementing capacity building activities as described above, NTA and the Ministry of Finance of Japan collaboratively develop a basic strategy, and manage the projects effectively.

Source: Japan's National Tax Agency.

Box 3.8. **Regional Focus for Capacity Building Efforts**

Hungary

Hungary's National Tax and Customs Administration (NTCA) prioritises neighbouring countries when selecting recipients for assistance. In particular, these efforts tend to focus on co-operation with Serbian and Ukrainian partner administrations, often in the context of different programmes financed by the European Union. For instance, in 2015, the NTCA participated in a Technical Assistance and Information Exchange (TAIEX) programme, financed by the European Union, with the Serbian partner administration.

Source: National Tax and Customs Administration, Hungary.

Slovenia

In accordance with the Government's strategy, Slovenia has prioritised countries from Southeast Europe for tax administration assistance. For instance, in recent years the Slovenian tax administration was involved in a project with Bosnia and Herzegovina and some bilateral assistance was delivered to Kosovo. In addition the Slovenian tax administration has been active in the EU FISCALIS programme where the training materials developed are made available to all participating countries.

Source: Financial Administration of the Republic of Slovenia.

Further, in view of the balance between bilateral and multilateral tax capacity building activities being carried out by FTA tax administrations, and given that many opportunities for peer-to-peer exchanges occur in the multilateral space, it bears noting that multilateral engagement forms an important, if not essential, component of a continuum for the building and enhancing of knowledge and abilities, as a precursor to implementation support. In this regard, it is important to emphasise that multilateral and bilateral activities are complementary: both are needed and have value, as tax administration practices demonstrate. An important consideration in setting out a delivery approach for these activities is in determining how they can be best deployed in the context of an assistance request. Building on a broad range of experience within the capacity building community, the following table highlights some of the benefits, as well as the drawbacks, of the two approaches.

Table 3.1. **Bilateral (one-to-one) versus multilateral (one-to-many) capacity building approaches**

Bilateral approaches		Multilateral approaches	
Benefits	**Drawbacks**	**Benefits**	**Drawbacks**
• High potential to tailor activities to needs • Broad reach within the host tax administrations • Better fit with organisational development programmes • More result oriented (when programme based)	• Risk of replication of past approaches without due adaption • May be more costly, especially for in-country secondment of experts • May create dependency, especially in case of long term in-country assignments • Smaller-scale interventions may may lack evaluation of impact, and therefore risk being incidental	• Allows for peer learning • Can be a less costly alternative • Stronger focus on personal development • Provides broader background and "state of the art" insights	• Can be difficult to select the right participants • Potential for limited impact (e.g. if too generic) • Less effective when no clear goal is set for participation • May be difficult to apply newfound knowledge and expertise in an operation setting
Application		**Application**	
• Good fit to support recipient administration in designing and implementing new strategies, especially when the administration lacks expert knowledge or programme management skills • Donor agency funded projects are more likely to benefit from internationally available shared body of knowledge and set of methodologies • Donor agency funded projects are more likely to benefit from independent review by or involvement of third parties such as other tax administrations or international bodies		• Good fit when introducing or encouraging reflections on approaches • Likely to be more effective when participating administrations are in similar circumstances e.g. regional groups • Important to make the activity part of participants' respective development programmes, to select the right participants and to ensure follow-up on outcomes	

Source: FTA Capacity Building Project Team.

A related issue that has long been a matter of debate is the relative value of short-term versus long-term technical assistance (STTA vs. LTTA). In fact, both approaches can be highly effective components of a comprehensive strategy for supporting tax reforms. Indeed, STTA and LTTA should be viewed as complementary parts of a flexible aid approach in which hands-on, practical LTTA builds capacity, with STTA topping it up through short-term missions and training. Acting on those insights, research undertaken by the IMF's Independent Evaluation Office in 2005 recommended a "life cycle model" for technical assistance as part of a long-term framework for institutional capacity development. The model cast LTTA as a key modality in countries with weak capacity, which included post conflict states. Then, as capacity improves, LTTA could be phased out in favour of short term missions and training (OECD and ITC, 2013).

Box 3.9. The importance of networking: New Zealand Inland Revenue's experience

New Zealand's Inland Revenue Department (NZIRD) participates in a wide range of capacity building activities with developing countries, much of which is focused on assisting small island developing states in the Pacific. In this context, assistance typically consists of providing expertise, through secondments of expert staff. Highlighting the importance of networking to support the effective implementation of capacity building assistance, the results of an external evaluation of tax reform in the Pacific has shown that, as it relates to NZIRD engagement with Samoa and the Solomon Islands, the secondment of staff can lead to networks that such countries can draw on for ongoing support. The report also acknowledges that the conclusion of a secondment can leave an expertise deficit in a recipient administration, and therefore suggests that, given the long-term nature of capacity building, donors should consider how they build a network of relationships which assist them to engage effectively in the ongoing dialogue between the donor and the host country.

Source: Sapere Research Group (2014).

In considering a delivery approach, a key issue is determining the "right" mix of activities to most effectively support the achievement of desired outcomes. As implied above, this "right" mix should be informed by the parameters established in a capacity building strategy and be relevant to the specific circumstances of a particular programme. In other words, meeting recipient administration needs is likely as dependent on effective delivery as substance.

Box 3.10. China's emphasis on training

As an OECD partner economy and a G20 member, China is an example of an emerging economy actively involved in the international tax dialogue (including for the BEPS project) but also one that relies upon the capacity building initiatives of developed countries given the limited resources of its tax authority, the State Administration of Taxation (SAT).

Currently, China and the OECD are working together to establish a new OECD-SAT Multilateral Tax Centre in China based on the SAT Multilateral Tax Center. This Centre will act as an important platform for the training of tax officials in China and from other developing countries. China has also sought to build its capacity through domestic initiatives including the development of a National Talent Training Programme. The objective of the programme is to develop a talent pool of one thousand people to further enhance China's tax administration. In this regard, China can be viewed as an example of a country doing more to put in place its own domestic capacity building framework.

Initiatives such as the talent programme combined with involvement with international (and regional) organisations has allowed China to improve areas of taxation that it believes are most important to its economy.

Source: China's State Administration of Taxation.

Resourcing

In the context of increasing demand for capacity building, coupled with its rising strategic relevance, FTA members have raised resourcing as a critical issue, as it relates to human resources as well as funding. With respect to human resources, most member country administrations have established a central unit for co-ordinating activities and/or managing relationships with international counterparts.

However, few donor tax administrations appear to have dedicated expert pools for capacity building activities. The HMRC's Tax Expert Unit, which is funded by resources made available by the national Department for International Development (DFID) to provide dedicated support to developing countries on G20/OECD tax priorities, appears to be the sole example of this type of structure.

Rather, for many, the resourcing of experts occurs on a case-by-case basis, meaning that they are drawn from tax programme areas as needed. Although there is consensus that the experience gained through participation in capacity building activities is beneficial to donor administration officials, for instance for career development purposes, these arrangements nevertheless present challenges that even funding cannot always address, as technical experts are not easy to replace. Perhaps for this reason, the use of long-term foreign deployments of tax administration staff appears to be rare among FTA member countries, with only a few tax administrations having these arrangements in place. In light of this, some FTA member countries suggest that there may be opportunities associated with leveraging retired experts; but, leveraging retirees is not without its challenges (e.g. identification, remuneration, currency of experience) and few actually do it. As a result, making greater use of retirees will likely first require further exploration of practical ways to tap into and manage this resource pool.

Box 3.11. **HMRC Tax Capacity Building Unit and Tax Expert Unit**

Using resources made available by the UK Department for International Development (DFID), HM Revenue and Customs (HMRC) has established a Tax Capacity Building Unit to deliver a 10 year programme of tax capacity building assistance, as well as a Tax Expert Unit to provide dedicated support to developing countries on G20/OECD tax priorities.

The Tax Capacity Building Unit was set up in 2013/14, to provide for:

- one-off short term missions (1-2 weeks) to address specific technical needs;
- longer-term missions, consisting of a number of short deployments (1-2 weeks) as part of a working partnership of 1-3 years; or
- secondments (2+ years) of an HMRC individual into a DFID country office to work directly with the host revenue authority to provide strategic advice and technical expertise, supported by short term missions (1-2 weeks).

The HMRC Tax Expert Unit was established in April 2015 to provide dedicated support to developing countries on G20/OECD international tax priorities. The Unit comprises four international tax and analytics experts who have significant expertise in a number of technical areas, including transfer pricing, BEPS and AEOI, who are able to work both bilaterally and with international multilateral organisations to provide technical assistance.

Source: HM Revenue and Customs, UK.

Likewise, few donor tax administrations appear to have long-term or core funding for their capacity building initiatives. While evidence suggests that tax administrations tend to be funded to execute projects on behalf of other institutional donors (e.g. national development agencies, European Union), costs associated with the provision of expertise outside a project context are generally ad-hoc and absorbed by the tax administration. An example of the former is the Dutch Tax and Customs Administration (DTCA), which has an agreement with the Dutch Ministry of Finance and the Dutch Ministry of Foreign Affairs, whereby funding is provided to cover the travel and daily allowance of DTCA staff members sent abroad. An example of the latter is the provision of tax administration experts to the OECD's Global Relations Programme, the costs of which tend to be absorbed by the donor tax administrations. Because insufficient funding can compromise the provision of support, it is therefore a key and critical issue that likely needs to be addressed more holistically and substantively in view of increasing demands for capacity building support.

Tracking and evaluation of impacts and results

Tracking and evaluating impacts and results is essential to effective assistance. It enables both the donor and the host tax administrations to assess the effectiveness of their efforts while also ensuring the commitment of participants to meaningful change; and, results can be used to support the planning of future capacity building programmes. In fact, the notion of "measuring progress and build(ing) the knowledge base on revenue matters" is the final of the OECD's principles for international engagement with developing countries on tax matters (OECD, 2013). There is little disagreement on the importance of these activities. In fact, formalised impact assessment and evaluation activities appear to be a fairly standard component of technical assistance projects, the presence of which is frequently a precondition of donor funding. For example, all projects funded by the European Union require an impact evaluation. Further, in the United Kingdom, a set of key performance indicators is established for each capacity building programme to track the results of activities against higher level objectives, with governance arrangements in place for each project, ensuring effective monitoring and reporting against each indicator. Finally, the importance of constructive feedback from host to donor administration should not be underestimated, and in fact, is an element embedded in some evaluation approaches; one such example being the methodology used by the United States Office of Technical Assistance (Box 3.12).

Still, notwithstanding the project-specific practices of some, the collective practice of tracking and evaluation appears far more fragmented. This means that on the whole there may be little evidence of what is being achieved. For instance, despite the investments donor tax administrations appear to make in collaborative exchange and training activities, few results appear to be tracked and where it is reported, it is not always clear as to the type of information produced and whether it is sufficient to make meaningful assessments of the impacts of activities. Although anecdotal, some donor tax administrations have observed that despite a great deal of training, recipient officials can still struggle when it comes to implementation. Coming full circle, it is to avoid these very circumstances that compel the use of a sound diagnostics, such as what is offered through TADAT, to drive a capacity building programme from the outset.

Box 3.12. United States Office of Technical Assistance

The mission of the Department of the Treasury's Office of Technical Assistance (OTA) is to help finance ministries and central banks of developing and transition countries strengthen their ability to manage public finances effectively and safeguard their financial sectors. Such assistance is in the interest of OTA partner countries and the United States.

Inception

OTA requires as a prerequisite to any potential engagement that a written request come from the foreign counterpart government.

Assessment

Where requested technical assistance is deemed to be within the OTA mandate, an on-the-ground assessment is typically conducted, in which OTA assessors meet with stakeholders to:

- determine whether technical assistance needs are consistent with the type of support OTA provides (e.g. consultative not equipment purchases);
- discuss the general goals and objectives of a prospective engagement; and
- assure that there is sufficient political will and leadership to make recommended reforms.

In the course of assessing the prospects for a given project, OTA also consults with other Treasury offices, and other U.S. government partners and stakeholders.

The assessment results and recommendations are detailed in a final written report. OTA recommendations to begin a new project are based on criteria and considerations that include:

- the need for technical assistance;
- evidence of counterpart commitment to reform and good use of assistance;
- whether the project would complement other projects in a particular country or region and not be duplicative;
- the relation of the project to Treasury policy priorities and broader U.S. Government goals; and
- the availability of funding.

Once a project is selected and a funding source identified, a Terms of Reference (TOR) document is presented to the counterpart agency and signed that describes the broad goals of the project. A detailed work plan is then developed which identifies key, prioritised challenges and the activities that will be undertaken to address them.

Staffing

Projects are led by an OTA advisor. OTA advisory are typically recruited and hired after having had established careers in relevant fields, and are supported by a small Washington-based office that provides management, administrative and logistical support. OTA maintains an ongoing recruitment process so that it can respond quickly and favourably to emerging counterpart needs.

Monitoring and evaluation

OTA evaluates its projects using a variety of methods, including:

- written monthly reports prepared by advisors that describe progress against work plan objectives;
- annual on-site programme reviews to meet with the counterparts and advisors, review the project progress, and support programmatic planning;

Box 3.12. **United States Office of Technical Assistance** *(continued)*

- end-of-tour report, which captures the feedback and assessment of advisors concluding a particular assignment as either a resident advisor or team lead in the case of an intermittent programme; and
- end-of-project report to evaluate the potential long-term impact of an engagement as well as to capture "lessons learned" to improve implementation elsewhere.

In addition to monitoring and evaluation through reporting, OTA also evaluates the "traction" and "impact" of its ongoing engagements through an annual exercise, done in accordance with U.S. government policy and guidance on programme evaluations. OTA also issues "customer" surveys to solicit feedback from policy and working-level counterparts in the host country, together with other interested parties.

Depending on the requirements of outside funders, OTA also prepares reporting documents that typically chronicle developments over a defined period (e.g. quarterly). These substantive reports are usually paired with financial reporting for that same duration.

Source: https://www.treasury.gov/about/organizational-structure/offices/Pages/Technical-Assistance-.aspx.

Bibliography

Addis Tax Initiative Declaration (2015), *Third International Conference on Financing for Development*, Addis Ababa, https://www.taxcompact.net/documents/Addis-Tax-Initiative_Declaration.pdf.

ITC and OECD (2015), *Examples of Successful DRM Reforms and the Role of International Co-operation*, Discussion Paper, www.oecd.org/ctp/tax-global/examples-of-successful-DRM-reforms-and-the-role-of-international-co-operation.pdf, Deutsche Gesellschaft für, Bonn.

NORAD Tax for Development, published 26 October 2011 and last updated 16 Feburary 2015, www.norad.no/en/front/thematic-areas/macroeconomics-and-public-administration/tax-for-development/.

OECD and International Tax Compact (ITC) (2013), *Tax and Development, Aid Modalities for Strengthening Tax Systems,* OECD Publishing, Paris, http://dx.doi.org/10.1787/9789264177581-en.

OECD (2013), *Principles for International Engagement in Supporting Developing Countries in Revenue Matters*, www.oecd.org/ctp/tax-global/Principles_for_international_engagement_May2013.pdf.

OECD (2015), *Tax Administration 2015: Comparative Information on OECD and Other Advanced and Emerging Economies*, OECD Publishing, Paris, http://dx.doi.org/10.1787/tax_admin-2015-en.

Sapere Research Group (2014), *Evaluation of Tax Reform in the Pacific*, Sapere Research Group, New Zealand.

TADAT (2015), *Field Guide*, www.tadat.org/files/IMF_TADAT-FieldGuide_web.pdf.

Chapter 4

Leveraging technology for tax capacity building

This chapter explores how leveraging technology can lead to more efficient and cost-effective delivery of capacity building support. It focuses on the broader application of technology, including e-learning types of approaches. It also provides a more in depth overview of the prototype Knowledge Sharing Platform, developed by Canada, which is a powerful online tool designed to promote, share, exchange and capture tax administration knowledge and expertise.

Given the peer-to-peer nature of tax administration support, it is not surprising that assistance typically has been, and continues to be, delivered in-person. Interaction is arguably a key ingredient of the knowledge sharing process, the importance of which likely increases in step with the degree of sophistication of a particular exchange. That said, as noted in the previous chapter, these efforts are constrained by resource availability, an issue that is taking on greater urgency in view of increasing demand – and one that calls for more efficient and smarter solutions in how elements of capacity building assistance can be delivered. Given the limited resources of tax administrations to undertake capacity building activities, leveraging collective knowledge and expertise will be critical.

Using technology to work smarter

Advances in technology, including the availability of web-based applications, present innovative and low-cost delivery options when compared to traditional delivery mechanisms for strengthening capacity, which can be resource intensive. Experience in other facets of tax administration – for example, service delivery – has shown that, where it makes sense, electronic delivery can satisfy demand in an efficient way. It stands to reason therefore that technology offers considerable potential as a delivery mechanism for capacity building activities. Accordingly, this chapter explores the value of leveraging technology, including e-learning tools, for capacity building purposes, and how it can be complemented and enhanced by the Knowledge Sharing Platform – a prototype global online tool, designed by and for tax administrations.

E-learning

For many tax administrations, new technologies have opened up new opportunities for innovative and efficient ways to build their technical capacity. Webinars, web-based interactive self-study or simulations, collaboration tools and community portals are integral elements of their overall training and learning strategies which offer employees access to a wide variety of resources geared to both formal and informal learning.

Such technologies, as well as more extensive use of social media and translation software, enable online types of learning (e-learning) that create new options for the development of capacity. Also, given the interactive capabilities of these web-based tools, there is considerable scope for efficiencies in how elements of capacity building are delivered.

While there will always be a place and need for classroom training, e-learning opens new opportunities to those who may otherwise be constrained from attending in-person events, for example due to high travel costs or inability to be away from the office for any significant period of time. Other advantages include:

- Uniform presentation of content;
- Self-paced study;
- Repeat access to material;
- Easy to update/upgrade.

While up-front development costs may be higher for online products, distribution costs are considerably lower and studies have concluded that online learning is as effective as classroom learning.

Box 4.1. **Canada: Tax audit fundamentals**

In 2007, the Canada Revenue Agency (CRA) developed, in collaboration with the Commonwealth Association of Tax Administrators, Tax Audit Fundamentals (TAF), an e-learning tool modelled on the CRA's classroom-based basic audit course. Adapted to an international audience, TAF was subsequently translated into French, Spanish and Portuguese and, thanks to further collaboration with CIAT and CREDAF, made available to tax administration officials in over 100 countries worldwide. TAF provides new auditors with a simple, easy to use tool to help build their audit skills from the comfort of their own office, and it continues to be used today.

Source: Canada Revenue Agency.

While many of these web-based applications are available and used by the tax administration community, others are underutilised (e.g. webinars) or non-existent (e.g. a multi-function knowledge sharing platform). Developing such e-learning based environments offers ample opportunities to create efficiencies and adopt approaches that are more tailored to individual needs.

Knowledge-sharing

With respect to knowledge-sharing, there are a number of useful websites hosted by a variety of organisations which offer a suite of resources for tax administrators. That said, access is often limited based on membership and, for tax administrations, there is no single platform that brings together information from multiple sources or connects the tax administration community globally.

This idea of using a technological platform for capacity building purposes with global reach is not new and has been employed with success in other fields. For example, the Electoral Knowledge Network, which offers a suite of services related to electoral knowledge, assistance and capacity development, has been a valuable asset to those involved in electoral capacity building.

Box 4.2. **Electoral Knowledge Network Practitioners' network**

The Electoral Knowledge Network practitioners' network is an online community of hundreds of election experts from around the world. The Network is a forum where electoral expertise, experience and knowledge can be shared. The aim of the practitioners' network is to promote the professionalism of the field of elections and to share knowledge resources with the general public. In order to fulfil these goals, the network provides an online space where election practitioners can interact, answer questions, provide peer advice, share and disseminate best practices, encourage new ideas, approaches and lessons learned.

Source: http://aceproject.org/about-en/practitioners2019-network.

Indeed, many organisations are already using websites to broaden access to tax administration materials; however, there are undoubtedly benefits and efficiencies to centralising access to these resources and providing additional functionalities to better enable efforts in these areas.

Recognising the benefits of leveraging technology, a number of tax administrations have already begun to explore and develop the use of technology as a tool for knowledge sharing. For example, Australia has developed a website for the SGATAR region (www.sgatar.org), to allow for exchange of ideas and best practices. Canada has also recently completed the development of a prototype online Knowledge Sharing Platform – to be discussed in the next section – to facilitate and promote the sharing of knowledge and expertise among tax administrations.

Knowledge Sharing Platform prototype

Developed and currently administered by Canada, the Knowledge Sharing Platform prototype has been designed as a global online tool to promote, share, exchange and capture knowledge and expertise. In its end state, such a Platform is intended for use by all interested tax administrations and international/regional tax organisations.

By design, the Platform is comprised of three complementary tiers intended to support, complement and optimise ongoing outreach and capacity building programmes:

- the library component, supporting self-study through e-learning and reference material while improving access and reducing duplication;
- the event management component, for training co-ordination and management as to streamline the learning experience, while driving efficiencies; and
- the communities of practice component, to enable ongoing virtual, interactive and cost-effective support.

These components extend across a system of "hubs" that can be created, branded, populated and managed by participating tax administrations or organisations. With this system, hub owners can reap common benefits without sacrificing autonomy. By design, the Platform will use an inclusive governance model including an "Editorial Board" to

Figure 4.1. **Knowledge sharing platform value proposition**

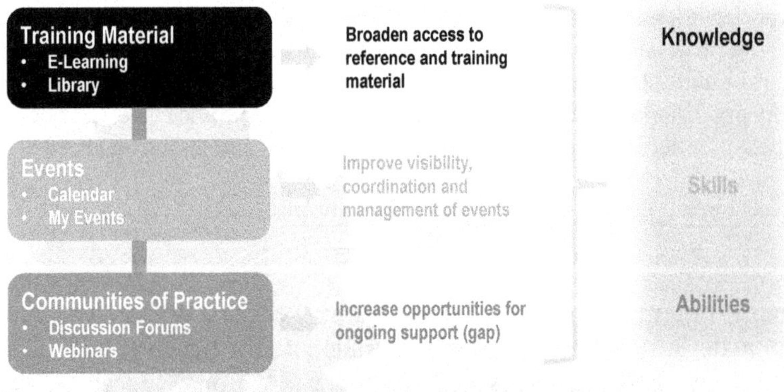

Source: Canada Revenue Agency (CRA).

help shape future development, including its co-ordinated management and curation of content. The Editorial Board will be composed of key stakeholder organisations and tax administrations.

Figure 4.2. **Knowledge Sharing Platform hub-based model**

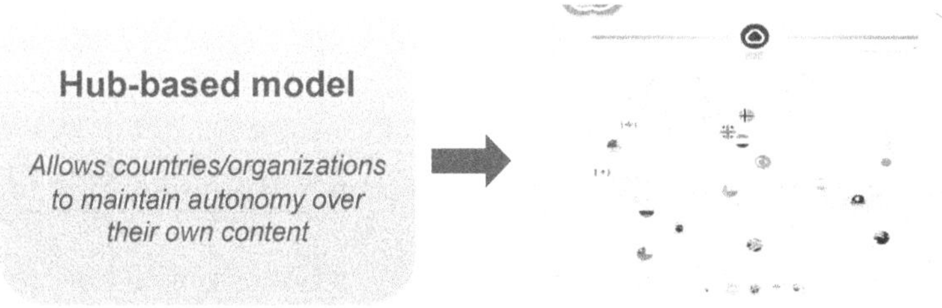

Source: Canada Revenue Agency (CRA).

In addition, the Knowledge Sharing Platform prototype has been designed to support a range of peer-to-peer technical assistance activities, providing integrated access to tools and materials. Moreover, with global reach, the Platform can also help facilitate broader knowledge sharing, for instance, south-south sharing of experiences and expertise by way of ongoing support, or through the sharing of post assessment insights, results, best practices as self-study reference material.

Several countries and organisations have signalled their interest and support for the Platform, with Canada currently conducting pilots with the Global Relations Programme, and with the Inter-American Centre of Tax Administrations (CIAT), to support the delivery to their respective activities. Moreover, developing countries also welcomed the creation of a Knowledge Sharing Platform, agreeing that it would provide a means to increase the efficiency of the Global Relations Programme and global co-operation in taxation (OECD, 2014:3). The Knowledge Sharing Platform prototype aims to improve access to support for tax administrations seeking assistance, whereas the providers of that support will be able to use it to help manage in-bound demand, across all tax topics including those related to BEPS and AEOI.

Through its core features (e.g. library, event management, and "communities of practice") the Knowledge Sharing Platform is designed to support, complement and optimise capacity building work. At the outset, the KSP holds great potential as a practical tool for widely disseminating the key outputs of the FTA's work programme (e.g. guidance on the implementation of BEPS and AEOI).

In the short-term, the prototype will be further developed and refined with a view to migrate to its ultimate end-state. Canada has committed to providing administrative support to the prototype for the next three to five years.

Bibliography

OECD (2014), *Summary of Outcomes by the Co-Chairs of the Advisory Group for Co-operation with Partner Economies*, www.oecd.org/tax/tax-global/AG-2014-Co-Chair-Outcomes-Summary.pdf.

The Electoral knowledge network (n.d.): http://aceproject.org/about-en/practitioners2019-network.

Tom Russell, The No Significant Difference Phenomenon, www.nosignificantdifference.org.

Chapter 5

Enhancing co-operation for tax capacity building

This chapter explores opportunities for tax administrations to work in more cohesive and strategic ways with stakeholders from the tax administration community and from various international and regional organisations.

While many countries, through their tax administration, development agency, or some combination thereof, have undertaken important capacity building work, much of this work is done in relative isolation and thereby may not benefit fully from the collective experience and tools that are available in the broader tax administration community. Increasing demands and commitments, in an environment with many actors and initiatives, call for greater coherence in how demand and supply for capacity building efforts are matched, including how peer-to-peer support is scoped and delivered.

Chapter 3 established the importance of sound processes to enable tax administrations to make informed interventions and investment decisions, while Chapter 4 explored options for broader, cost-effective delivery of assistance. However, while a gap analysis appears to be routine in the development of a bilateral assistance programmes, a similar "gap analysis" appears to be lacking in the context of tax administrations' collective support to capacity building efforts. Currently, there is little available to tax administrations to help determine where their efforts could be used to best effect, relative to and in consideration of, the work of others across the institutional landscape. Unfortunately, the absence of a framework to guide and situate capacity building work sets the stage for potential overlaps and gaps in assistance. A more structured approach to international co-ordination holds the promise of adding value to domestic efforts avoiding duplication and better identifying best practices. Accordingly, this chapter explores opportunities for tax administrations to work in more cohesive and strategic ways with other stakeholders, both within the tax administration community, and within the broader collectivity of stakeholders.

Co-ordination among donor tax administrations

The experience of some FTA member countries suggests that the effective and efficient delivery of assistance can be complicated or have reduced impact due to other actors providing duplicate or competing assistance. Co-ordination among donor tax administrations is therefore important in this context, and in fact, is embedded in the OECD's principles for international engagement with developing countries on tax matters, which notes that "international partners have the responsibility to organise their assistance in a harmonised way, with an agreed division of labour, using appropriate co-ordination and dialogue mechanisms at the country level" (OECD, 2013).

Box 5.1. **BRICS countries' commitment to tax capacity building co-operation**

At the 3rd meeting of BRICS' Heads of Tax Authorities (19-20 November 2015), Commissioners from BRICS countries reached a consensus on deepening the co-operation within BRICS and with other international and regional organisations to optimise existing capacity building resources and maximise the effect of technical assistance to developing countries.

Source: Communiqué of BRICS Heads of Revenue Meeting issued in Moscow on 19 November, 2015.

With greater co-ordination, the collective effort of tax administrations in delivering assistance that matches recipient needs in a timely manner should also improve. The factors that lead donor administrations to contribute to certain requests for assistance over others raises the possibility of imbalances in the receipt of assistance, in that some developing countries may have more opportunities to benefit from assistance activities while others enjoy less. Ensuring a more level playing field in this regard is particularly crucial in view of the G20 agenda, which is reliant on a co-ordinated and coherent response in which all countries can engage. Thus, a more strategic approach taken by tax administrations to network, co-ordinate, co-operate, and collaborate will help accomplish goals not achievable by working in isolation. Working together will also better position tax administrations to deal with a greater proportion of the demand.

Box 5.2. **South Africa's collaboration with others to deliver assistance**

The South African Revenue Service (SARS) is actively involved in supporting tax capacity building through:

- bilateral engagement of technical officers;
- exchange of experts on identified topics;
- hosting visits on request; and
- implementing technical assistance projects in the area of exchange of information and audit.

SARS has partnered with other FTA members to deliver certain technical assistance projects. For instance, SARS collaborated with the Netherlands to deliver support to Kenya on exchange of information. Likewise, SARS partnered with Sweden to support Malawi and Rwanda to build audit capacity. SARS also provides experts to the African Tax Administration Forum (ATAF) which reaches a cross-continental audience in a variety of topics during capacity building events.

Source: South African Revenue Service.

Even so, it is important to be aware that tax administrations' collective efforts most likely cannot fully meet all demand. Therefore, initiatives led by multilateral international organisations, such as the IMF, the World Bank, the OECD (e.g. Global Relations Programme, Tax Inspectors Without Borders (with the UN)), and regional organisations can be helpful to assess and fill gaps in support.

Research undertaken for this study shows that FTA member countries have been near universal in their calls for strengthened co-ordination and reduced duplication, so it follows that a move by the FTA in this direction would meet a need and be welcomed. To put into practice the identification and tracking of programmes and initiatives, including peer-to-peer activities and the relationships between them could be a useful first step to help decrease duplication of effort while also fostering co-operative work among donor tax administrations. Further, if made broadly available, such an inventory of activity could highlight the assistance donor administrations can offer to developing countries, promoting the various assistance programmes and their relevance for different countries.

Bringing the donor tax administration community together also offers a parallel opportunity to improve tracking and evaluation of results – a key issue identified by donor tax administrations – by aggregating individual practices to build collective expertise around the factors that contribute to success. For instance, identifying and cataloguing measures and inviting countries that have embarked on significant capacity-building efforts to describe their experiences could help tax administrations (and donor agencies) determine where to engage, generally, and in the context of specific priorities such as BEPS implementation.

Box 5.3. **Partnerships with regional tax organisations**

Finland

The Finnish Tax Administration is actively working with the African Tax Administration Forum (ATAF) to deliver targeted technical assistance, mostly to the Namibian Inland Revenue Department to build capacity in the Large Taxpayers Unit. The focus of this work is on risk analysis, client relations management and tax audit capabilities, including the first steps on transfer pricing operations. Although the capacity building project will make use of resources of the Finnish Tax Administration and is funded by the Finnish Ministry on Foreign Affairs, the assistance is provided by ATAF as a part of their technical assistance programme.

Source: Finnish Tax Administration.

Mexico

Mexico has been part of the Inter-American Centre of Tax Administration (CIAT) since its founding in 1965. In this context, Mexico's tax administration service – the Servicio de Administración Tributaria (SAT) – has been appointed President of CIAT's Executive Council four times (1969, 1981, 1990, 2003). In 2016, Mexico hosted CIAT's 50th General Assembly in order to enhance and strengthen multilateral fiscal co-operation in Latin America and the Caribbean.

Some of Mexico's technical assistance programmes are undertaken as part of official co-operation between the SAT and CIAT. For instance, recent support from Mexico to CIAT member countries has included the following:

- technical assistance on transfer pricing, mutual agreement procedures and taxation of hydrocarbons provided to Trinidad and Tobago;
- technical assistance on risk management to Ecuador;
- technical assistance on transfer pricing, international audits, and taxpayer services to China; and
- technical assistance on exchange of information, and legal framework regarding FATCA, to Panama.

Events are delivered by SAT officials in SAT facilities, typically over a three-day period, with logistics covered by CIAT and recipient tax administrations. With CIAT support, SAT has also received the following technical assistances:

- technical assistance on Advanced Transfer Pricing Agreements, provided by the General Direction of Public Finance of France; and
- technical assistance on risk management, provided by the Tax Administration of India.

From 2015 to the date, SAT has offered 140 educational grants for 20 academic programmes from CIAT related to transfer pricing, exchange of information, tax audits, customs and tax collection.

Source: Servicio de Administración Tributaria, Mexico.

Connecting the FTA to the work of others

The previous section touched on the notion of a more coherent approach to assistance provided by tax administrations. Given that donor tax administrations have observed some gaps between the implementation challenges that host tax administrations face and the training and assistance that is currently provided, the issue of coherence likely has relevance in the context of the institutional landscape as well. Although the scope of this study did not allow for (nor intend) a comprehensive diagnostic of the assistance and support available to tax administrations, it can nevertheless be said that developing relationships with the intent to work with and through other organisations can help manage demand, reduce duplication and build synergies in delivery.

The role of the FTA in facilitating the exchange of best practices and sharing of experiences is core to its mandate and is a key strength. In view of key domestic and cross-border tax challenges faced by developing countries, the FTA has an opportunity to calibrate the substance of its work programme efforts and outputs to support capacity building. By extension, it follows that there is value for the FTA in considering where and how it can extend its reach in the dissemination of reports and tools for effective tax administration.

Further, within the FTA, the notion that there are opportunities for the FTA to support, complement and optimise the work of others enjoys broad consensus, with members seeing significant value in co-ordinating and aligning FTA efforts within the community to support the broader international capacity building agenda on topics that affect all tax administrations, including BEPS implementation and the further advancement of the G20 agenda. How the FTA can achieve synergies with international organisations in the context of their platform for collaboration on tax is one such example of where exploration of opportunities is likely warranted. That said, any such work in this space will need to be carried out in a way that is mindful of the mandate and membership of the FTA, specifically that the FTA largely represents donor tax administrations, whose role is to support capacity building initiatives through the provision of expertise.

To illustrate the potential in this regard, Figure 5.1 shows a selection of the FTA's key relationships or involvement with other organisations and initiatives.

Table 5.1. **Examples of co-operation between organisations**

Phase of assistance	Organisations involved	Area(s) of co-operation
Programme development/ Evaluation	IMF/WB via TADAT	• Diagnostics (assessment/reassessment)
	IMF/OECD/RTOs via RA-FIT	• Data capture, monitoring and comparison
Delivery	RTOs	• Awareness (including through BEPS toolkits) • Training (online and in-person) • Assistance
	OECD GRP	• Dialogue/Training
	Global Forum	• Technical assistance
	IMF/OECD/UNDP/WBG	• Technical assistance

Source: FTA Capacity Building Project Team.

Figure 5.1. **FTA members' footprint with selected organisations and initiatives**

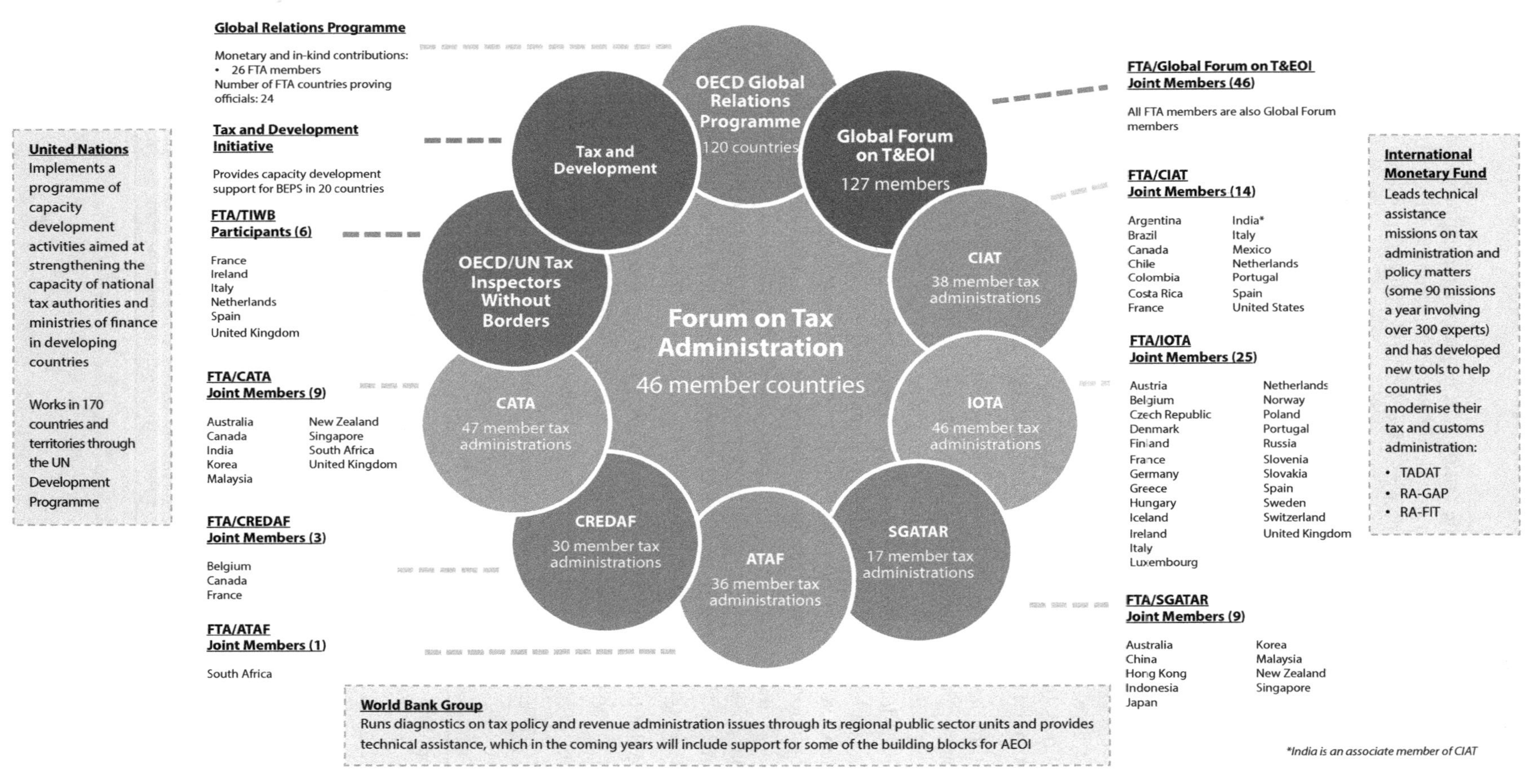

Source: FTA Capacity Building Project Team.

Further examination of the range of existing relationships between the FTA and other organisations (see Table 5.1) reveals an alignment with the notion of a structured, comprehensive approach to capacity building as was introduced in Chapter 3.

Considering relationships in a structured way can help pinpoint opportunities for closer, constructive and efficient collaboration going forward. As an example, by way of existing relationships the FTA is well positioned to contribute and align administrative considerations within existing training and knowledge sharing programmes offered by other institutions. For instance, the FTA's current work on BEPS, specifically the use of country-by-country reporting, which is being developed for FTA members, could also form the basis for more universal consultation and guidance that in turn could be disseminated widely though other institutions. However, this is but one example. Further and ongoing exploration of the full suite of potential opportunities – along with a mechanism to do so – will be needed to realise the greatest benefits.

Bibliography

BRICS Heads of Revenue, *Communiqué of BRICS Heads of Revenue Meeting*, Moscow, 19 November 2015, http://en.brics2015.ru/load/795871.

OECD (2013), *Draft Principles for International Engagement in Supporting Developing Countries in Revenue Matters*, www.oecd.org/ctp/tax-global/Principles_for_international_engagement_May2013.pdf.

Chapter 6

The tax administration capacity building framework

In view of key challenges facing donor tax administrations with respect to their capacity building efforts, this chapter proposes a preliminary conceptual framework to assist with both individual and collective identification, planning, sequencing and evaluation of initiatives.

This study has revealed a number of key challenges facing donor tax administrations with respect to capacity building efforts. Key among them are:

- a lack of co-ordination, including difficulties in ensuring a cohesive, strategic way of working with other stakeholders;
- limited or underutilised structures and tools to make informed decisions on where and how to invest for best effect, so that ultimately host administration officials can fully capitalise on the assistance received;
- notwithstanding a few exceptions, the absence of core or long-term funding, which has resource implications and diminishes donor tax administrations' ability to respond to demand for capacity building assistance; and
- sustainable mechanisms to ensure the delivery of assistance in a balanced and broader way, to the benefit of the collective tax administration community overall.

As a means to begin to address these challenges, donor tax administrations would benefit from considering a common approach and/or complementary view of capacity building assistance. Increasing demands and commitments call for a more coherent approach to capacity building support – one that, at a minimum, considers the relative value of a given activity, programme or initiative, and provides some foundational parameters for more informed decision-making on where and how to target and invest resources – not only for tax administrations in their individual capacity but also among the collective community of support providers. Tax administration experience already suggests an implicit structure, which starts with the notion of a needs assessment and concludes with an assessment of results, with a logical and progressive sequence of activities in between to build the knowledge, skills and abilities of tax officials. This would be a logical starting point for the development of any common approach.

To begin to address the need for greater coherence and commonality in the organisation and delivery of peer-to-peer support, Figure 6.1 proposes a preliminary conceptual framework

Figure 6.1. **The tax administration capacity building framework**

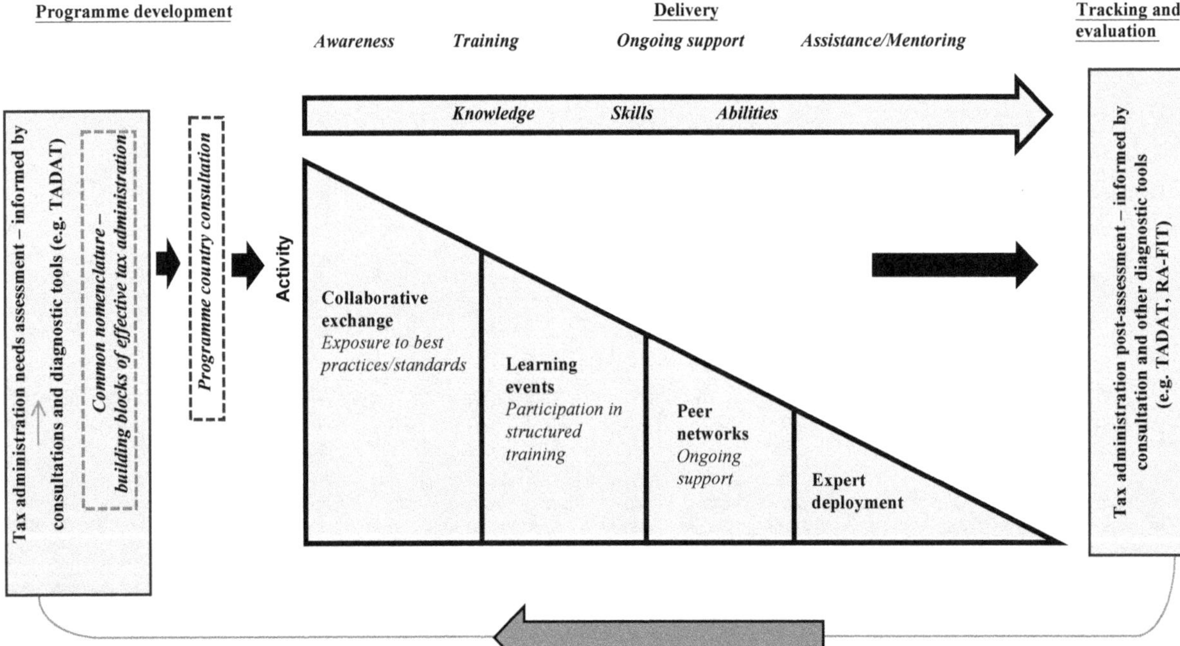

Source: FTA Capacity Building Project Team.

that combines the elements noted above: a programme development approach based on diagnostics; a common nomenclature that articulates the core building blocks of taxation; delivery through a sequence of complementary activities, relevant to any of the core building blocks; and the embedding of results tracking and evaluation.

By its design, the framework translates several key principles into a concrete process. These principles include:

- **The programme development process needs begin with sound diagnostics.** The notion that effective capacity building targets areas of priority – identified by host governments – has as its reciprocal that tax administrations should focus their efforts and investments where there is an identified need, and where the request for assistance has merit and is feasible. To the extent possible, tax administrations should set as an objective the use of common diagnostic tools to bring greater focus to international efforts. Having been developed with broad international input and support, the Tax Administration Diagnostic Assessment Tool (TADAT) offers good potential to elevate practice in this area.
- **A common approach requires a common nomenclature.** Having a standard way to describe and define the core building blocks of taxation to which tax administrations can relate and precisely situate their work enables the shared understanding and means of communication among stakeholders that must underpin a common approach. It can also form the basis for further improvements, for instance, in how performance data is collectively tracked and compared.
- **Sophisticated interventions have best effect if a certain threshold of capacity is established first**, to ensure interventions can be successful and sustained. Care therefore needs to be taken to ensure that capacity building activities are undertaken in a sequence that is relevant to a given recipient's readiness to implement reforms and sustain outcomes. In this regard, the framework suggests a broad progression of four activity types that progressively build knowledge, skills and abilities. Three of the four activity types – exchange of best practices, training, and expert deployment – are fairly common and time-tested tools. A fourth – ongoing support through peer networks – likely has been underutilised despite its potential value.
- **Tracking and evaluating results is vital**, not only for assessing effectiveness but also for informing the development of future capacity building activities, to replicate successes and mitigate the risks associated with sub-optimal outcomes. Available tools offer a good starting point in this regard. For instance, where TADAT is used to assess needs at the outset, it can also be used gauge progress through repeat assessments. Likewise, RA-FIT offers a common platform for the capture and sharing of data on key indicators. At the same time, the importance of qualitative data, such as feedback from host to donor administrations, should not be underestimated, nor should the utility of mid-point measurement.

For illustrative purposes, this conceptual framework can be taken one step further, to show the universality of the approach, regardless of delivery approach, or topic i.e. "building block". Further, as the expertise tax administrations can offer to developing countries is broader than the technical aspects of tax, there is potential to expand and deepen this framework to include all issues relevant to the effective running of a tax administration. Ultimately, a more advanced framework should be applicable to the broadest spectrum of assistance that tax administrations can provide.

Figure 6.2. **The tax administration capacity building framework**

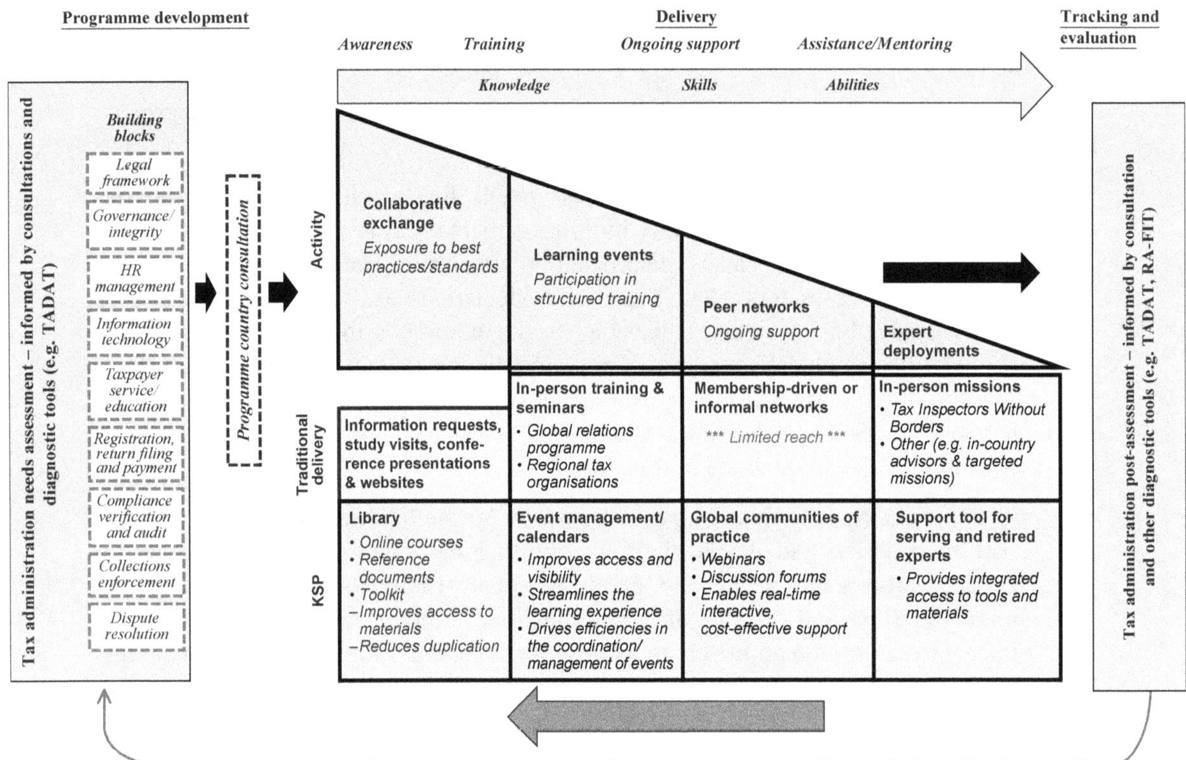

Source: FTA Capacity Building Project Team.

Chapter 7

Observations and recommendations

Drawing on the findings of the report, this chapter summarises several key observations which preface the four recommendations that provide practical guidance as to how the FTA and its members can best organise themselves to contribute to capacity building efforts in a co-ordinated, cost-effective and sustainable way.

The results of the FTA Capacity Building Project mapping exercise and survey of member countries show that FTA members play a key role in supporting capacity building efforts. However, the capacity of tax administrations to support these efforts is not infinite and must be reconciled with competing demands. The increasing gap between demands and commitments highlights the need for a coherent and common approach that provides, at a minimum, some foundational parameters within which to consider issues and, over time, yield better investment decisions and more sustainable outcomes.

Observations

The results of the FTA Capacity Building Project have revealed several important observations:

- **International co-operation is vital and of strategic importance to tax administrations.** In an increasingly integrated international tax system, engagement with those beyond the FTA is mutually beneficial and core to the effectiveness of global tax administration. Looking towards the implementation of the G20 priorities, including the implementation of BEPS and AEOI in the next years, will require a co-operative and inclusive approach. In this regard, FTA member countries encourage and welcome the participation of developing country administrations in capacity building efforts, and further, see strategic value in extending the reach of the FTA.
- **FTA member countries play a key role in supporting capacity building efforts**, both through their engagement in the international and regional tax organisations and via the provision of bilateral support to developing country tax administrations. The challenge in developing more robust strategies for capacity building is paramount. To effectively deliver capacity building assistance, well-defined policies with regard to partnerships and long term commitments, selection of programmes, types of assistance, necessary skills and expertise and programme evaluation are needed.
- **How donor tax administrations organise for capacity building influences the achievement of meaningful outcomes and efficiencies.** The findings in this report suggest that tax administrations' efforts in capacity building are most impactful and efficient when:
  - Tax administrations consider capacity building to be a strategic issue. For donor tax administrations, capacity building strategies that prioritise this kind of support, in line with agreed timetables and commitments (e.g. such as to the agreed minimum standards) and with due regard for broader capacity building needs, can help focus attention where it is most needed.
  - Capacity building efforts are delivered taking a whole-of-government approach. Convinced of the merits of this approach, several jurisdictions are already exploring its practical application. The successful implementation of whole-of-government approaches is likely to elevate the standard of best practice for how countries organise themselves to achieve more effective and sustainable results.
  - Capacity building follows a programme-based approach. In this regard, the conceptual framework introduced in chapter 6 provides a common reference to help guide the delivery efforts of tax administrations.
  - Delivery aligns with recipient needs. The "right" mix of activities is informed by the parameters established in a capacity building strategy and is relevant to the specific circumstances of a particular programme.

  - The availability of core or long-term funding enables tax administrations to organise their capacity building efforts on a more structured instead of on an ad hoc basis.
  - Implementation is supported by sufficient tracking and evaluation of impacts and results. Tax administrations can benefit from the development and implementation of sound and consistent diagnostics as a basis to systematically plan and evaluate their capacity building activities.

- **The increasing demand for capacity building, and the extent to which it draws on scarce knowledge and skills, compel tax administrations to work smarter in delivering assistance.** Although there is considerable variety in how assistance efforts are organised and executed, budget and resourcing constraints are a common impediment to FTA members' capacity to meet accelerating demand for tax administration support. There is broad support among FTA members for innovation in how capacity building is delivered, including through technology. Drawing more on e-learning type of solutions and advancing the options for knowledge sharing – such as the via the Knowledge Sharing Platform – can serve as complementary enabling environment and support tools, both generally and in relation to BEPS and AEOI implementation assistance.
- **The value and application of a common approach to capacity building assistance merits further exploration.** The FTA is well positioned to begin these deliberations, by drawing on the experiences of its member countries, along with their respective relationships with other developing country administrations and/or institutional stakeholders. In this regard, momentum will need to be built and sustained.

Recommendations

The role of the FTA in facilitating the exchange of best practices and sharing of experiences is core to its mandate and is a key strength. This certainly is relevant in the domain of tax administration capacity building, where FTA member countries' efforts are key to achieve sustainable results in strengthening tax administration.

This report offers four key recommendations to guide the early efforts of the FTA and its member countries. Taken together, these recommendations provide guidance as to how the FTA and its member countries can best organise themselves to contribute to capacity building efforts in a co-ordinated, cost-effective and sustainable way.

While these recommendations will help tax administration meet demand, they also better position FTA member countries to support the implementation of the BEPS and AEOI, hallmarks of the G20 tax agenda that seek to strengthen the integrity of the global tax system. Going forward, the FTA will focus efforts on engaging member countries with a view to advancing these recommendations.

1. **That the FTA and its members adopt and advance a common Tax Administration Capacity Building Framework.**

This report suggests a common framework as the basis to inform both domestic and international dialogues and strategies of tax administrations. The framework introduced in Chapter 6, while conceptual, is consistent with long-standing international development approaches and is intended as an early iteration of such a practical guide to assist with both individual and collective identification, planning, sequencing and evaluation of initiatives.

For the FTA and its member countries, a common view of the capacity building landscape – guided by the conceptual framework – could help shed light of where the FTA's collective efforts and investments can be brought to bear with most effect and bring about other practical benefits such as:

- clarity on what support is currently available;
- better identification of gaps and overlaps in assistance and support;
- determination of areas of complementarity between the work of tax administrations and others; and
- the identification of opportunities for new (or renewed) partnerships.

2. **That the FTA and its members help strengthen domestic efforts in capacity building by seeking to apply a "whole-of-government" approach.**

Recognising the merits of domestic co-operation, the OECD, through its Tax and Development Programme, has already established the application of whole-of-government approaches as one of ten key principles for effective delivery of support to developing countries in revenue matters. This principle was recently reaffirmed through the Addis Declaration where signatories committed to adhering to these principles. Countries that have shown leadership in this area have begun integrating tax administration activities to development programming and have recognised the benefits of doing so.

In a whole-of-government context, alongside development agencies and finance departments, tax administrations are uniquely positioned to provide expertise across the entire tax administration spectrum and they typically have an inherent understanding of the culture of tax administrations (United Kingdom House of Commons, 2012-2013: 27). Moreover, in working together with development agencies, tax administrations would stand to benefit from their well-established development experience and "on the ground" network given their membership in numerous communities that provide for sustained relationships beyond those typically associated with projects or initiatives. More generally, by sharing their respective expertise and resources, domestic partners engaged in whole-of-government approaches would shape more focused and sustainable capacity building efforts.

3. **That the FTA and its members participate in the development of the Knowledge Sharing Platform.**

Options that allow for cost-effective delivery and broadened reach are a necessary part of the way forward for tax administrations. Appetite is strong among FTA members for innovation in how knowledge is shared and used to support capacity building, with general consensus around the benefits of leveraging technology to foster closer co-operation with others and to create efficiencies in sharing expertise to support capacity development.

The Knowledge Sharing Platform prototype has been designed with these objectives in mind and is intended for use by all interested tax administrations, including developing country tax administrations, and international and regional tax organisations.

Further, it is also recommended that the FTA, as a key Knowledge Sharing Platform partner, would participate in the governance of the Knowledge Sharing Platform by joining its "Editorial Board" to help shape the Platform's future development, including its co-ordinated management and curation of content.

4. **That the FTA establishes a Capacity Building Network to connect to the work of others.**

With greater co-ordination, the collective effort of tax administrations in delivering assistance that matches recipient needs can improve. This is crucial in view of the G20 agenda, which is shaped around BEPS and AEOI, and reflects the common concern and top priorities of the international community, with the robust implementation of both recognised as essential to the integrity of the international tax system and the sustainable mobilisation of domestic resource for donor and host countries. A number of initiatives are currently underway that have resulted in unprecedented co-operation among international and regional organisations. While some FTA members are part of these organisations and initiatives, more could be done to connect the FTA and its members to support and complement these efforts.

Accordingly, this report recommends that the FTA establish a Capacity Building Network that will be tasked with better connecting the efforts of the FTA and its member countries to the work of others to both mitigate the risks of gaps and overlaps and identify areas where a more co-ordinated approach could produce mutual and tangible benefits.

At the outset, under the leadership of the FTA sponsoring commissioners and the support of the FTA Secretariat, the Network will:

- Lead work to further refine the Capacity Building Framework, thereby advancing the first recommendation. This includes the further development of guidance and sharing of best practices that can support a programme-based approach as set out in this report.
- Establish and strengthen partnerships with other organisations and programmes by further developing the relationship between the FTA and key stakeholders including international organisations and regional organisations; this will entail developing mechanisms to draw on the expertise of other institutions, e.g. as related to diagnostics and measurement of results and developing arrangements or mechanisms to deploy experts as a means of practical support to TIWB; and
- Explore methods that could support better co-ordination with other organisations, including consideration of mechanisms for tracking or reporting on the respective capacity building activities undertaken by participating FTA member countries, and for the cataloguing of experts.

Bibliography

United Kingdom House of Commons, 2012-2013, *Tax in Developing Countries: Increasing Resources for Development*, Internal Development Committee of the United Kingdom House of Commons (Fourth Report of Session 2012-13), www.publications.parliament.uk/pa/cm201213/cmselect/cmintdev/130/130vw.pdf, London.

ORGANISATION FOR ECONOMIC CO-OPERATION AND DEVELOPMENT

The OECD is a unique forum where governments work together to address the economic, social and environmental challenges of globalisation. The OECD is also at the forefront of efforts to understand and to help governments respond to new developments and concerns, such as corporate governance, the information economy and the challenges of an ageing population. The Organisation provides a setting where governments can compare policy experiences, seek answers to common problems, identify good practice and work to co-ordinate domestic and international policies.

The OECD member countries are: Australia, Austria, Belgium, Canada, Chile, the Czech Republic, Denmark, Estonia, Finland, France, Germany, Greece, Hungary, Iceland, Ireland, Israel, Italy, Japan, Korea, Luxembourg, Mexico, the Netherlands, New Zealand, Norway, Poland, Portugal, the Slovak Republic, Slovenia, Spain, Sweden, Switzerland, Turkey, the United Kingdom and the United States. The European Union takes part in the work of the OECD.

OECD Publishing disseminates widely the results of the Organisation's statistics gathering and research on economic, social and environmental issues, as well as the conventions, guidelines and standards agreed by its members.

OECD PUBLISHING, 2, rue André-Pascal, 75775 PARIS CEDEX 16
(23 2016 19 1 P) ISBN 978-92-64-25662-0 – 2016

www.ingramcontent.com/pod-product-compliance
Lightning Source LLC
LaVergne TN
LVHW081421110826
845149LV00010B/1824
* 9 7 8 9 2 6 4 2 5 6 6 2 0 *